Lives for Sale

The Biographers, a satirical engraving showing Hester Piozzi,
John Courtenay and James Boswell at work on their biographies of
Samuel Johnson, with Johnson's bust looking down disapprovingly.

Lives for Sale

Biographers' Tales

Edited by

Mark Bostridge

continuum
LONDON • NEW YORK

Continuum
The Tower Building
11 York Road
London SE1 7NX

15 East 26th Street
New York
NY 10010

www.continuumbooks.com

'Breaking In' by Andrew Motion was originally published in Granta 41, *Biography*, in 1992.
'Confessions of a Long-Distance Biographer' by Robert Skidelsky first appeared in the *Independent on Sunday* in November 2003.

First published 2004

British Library Cataloguing-in-Publication Data
A catalogue record for this book is available from the British Library.

ISBN 0 8264 7573 6

Typeset by Kenneth Burnley, Wirral, Cheshire
Printed and bound by Cromwell Press Ltd, Trowbridge, Wilts

To the memory of
Frances Partridge
(1900–2004)
A friend to biographers

And for
Oliver Bostridge
A joy to one biographer in particular

I confess, the subject is but dull in itself, to tell the time and places of men's birth, and deaths, their names, with the names and number of their books: and therefore this bare skeleton of time, place and person must be fleshed with some pleasant passages. To this intent I have purposely interlaced (not as meat, but as condiment) many delightful stories.

Thomas Fuller, *The Worthies of England* (1662)

Contents

x   *Contents*

Preface

Biography is a peculiarly British vice. In no other country is it such a staple feature of publishing schedules, bookshops and literary supplements. There may be continuing debate about whether it is a branch of history or literature, whether it should primarily be a work of record or an imaginative exercise, or how precisely the biographer can attain a balance between the two; but the appeal of the form remains in essence the same as that sketched out by Samuel Johnson, himself the subject of the most famous biography in the language, in his essay 'On the Genius of Biography' in *Rambler* No. 60, in 1750. Johnson, who once proclaimed his love of biography by saying that he could write 'The Life of a Broomstick', wrote that 'No species of writing . . . can more certainly enchain the heart by irresistible interest, or more widely diffuse instruction to every diversity of condition . . . We are all prompted by the same motives, all deceived by the same fallacies, all animated by hope, obstructed by desire, and seduced by pleasure.'

The history of English literature is filled with a long and proud tradition of life writing, all the way from the exemplary and moralistic to the critical and iconoclastic. From Cavendish and Roper's lives of Wolsey and More, Walton's pious biographies of Donne and Herbert – perhaps the earliest biographical work to possess real literary merit – and Aubrey's scurrilous anecdotage, through Johnson and Boswell, we move to the earnestness of the Victorian *Life and Letters*, and then to Strachey, standard bearer for the new biography of the 1920s, with its accent on irony and astringency. The list could be endless.

In our own time, modern biography is often said to date from 1967, and the publication of the first volume of Michael Holroyd's life of Lytton Strachey which broke through the barriers of biographical discretion by setting out to treat Strachey's homosexuality 'without any artificial veils of decorum': to write, in other words, of homosexuality just as one would of heterosexuality. But it was not just the details of Strachey's sexual life that stirred up controversy. Far more disturbing was the revelation of Maynard Keynes's homosexuality, which his official biographer, Roy Harrod, had explicitly denied. 1967 was the year in which Richard Nixon was making speeches saying that 'We are all Keynesians now.' With Holroyd's disclosures, Nixon's statements took on a whole new meaning. And, as Holroyd recalls, one critic went so far as to describe his book as a danger to the Western world.

Lives for Sale is a collection of new and anecdotal essays by many of the finest biographers writing in Britain at the beginning of the twenty-first century. Here are not only the established names, but also the rising stars of the profession – literary, historical and political biographers, biographers of artists and explorers. These are biographers' tales of the ups and downs of life writing: of shocking discoveries and frustrating dead ends, strange literary hauntings and curses, bitter professional rivalries, and of ways in which the biographical imagination can be aroused by a sense of place or the touch of a letter. Essays in favour of biography, or which speak up for the beleaguered practitioner, who has sometimes been attacked as a scoundrel (biographers were 'a disease of English literature' according to George Eliot); others which express disenchantment with attempts to capture another human being in the pages of a book.

The occasion for the appearance of this new collection is the publication, in September 2004, of the *Oxford Dictionary of*

National Biography [*Oxford DNB*], the largest co-operative research project ever undertaken in the humanities, and the most extensive new publishing project of the new century so far. Its statistics are impressive and awe-inspiring. Sixty volumes in print and online, covering 2,400 years of British history; over 50,000 biographies amounting to 60 million words, written by 10,000 contributors, and with the bonus of 10,000 illustrations. Brian Harrison, who succeeded the late Colin Matthew as editor of the *Oxford DNB* in January 2000, writes in 'The Dictionary Man' on page 76 of his personal experience of managing this gigantic enterprise. Many of the biographers in *Lives for Sale* have contributed to the new dictionary.

Of course, 'capsule' biography of the type practised by both the original *DNB* and its successor – the requirement to summarize a life in a short essay – rather than 'tombstone' biography, the weighty tomes that have become increasingly common since the 1960s, brings a different set of problems in its wake. Sidney Lee, who co-edited the *DNB* with its first editor Leslie Stephen before assuming overall responsibility as sole editor, likened the individual biographer to 'a painter transferring a great building to canvas', whereas the national biographer 'resembles the draftsman of an architectural elevation'. Nonethless, the *DNB* faced on a large scale many of the problems of individual biography. For instance, it fought similar battles over matters of discretion, as well as having to ensure that eulogy was kept within bounds ('No flowers by request' as Tennyson's friend, the writer and humorist Alfred Ainger put it). Nor was the *DNB* 'dryasdust' – far from it. How could it be with an editor like Stephen, who enlivened his own articles with such fascinating ephemera as the weight of Thackeray's brain (58 $\frac{1}{2}$ ounces), and Wordsworth's height (exactly 5' 9 $\frac{7}{8}$" tall); or who included an incongruous anecdote to lend colour to a serious subject like David Hume

(Hume, Stephen wrote, 'had grown very fat, and was once rescued by an old woman from a bog into which he had fallen on condition of repeating the Creed and the Lord's Prayer')?

The remarkable extent of the publishing achievement of the *DNB*, in quarterly instalments between 1885 and 1901, is perhaps indicative of our national obsession with biography. As one reviewer noted in 1901, 'Our British lexicographers have had the satisfaction of administering a handsome beating to their most formidable competitors, the Germans. Their dictionary in forty-five volumes took twenty-five years to waddle through the alphabet; our own, with its sixty-three, trotted the distance . . . in fifteen years and a half.' The *DNB* owed its existence to George Smith, publisher of the Brontës, George Eliot, Mrs Gaskell and Browning, among others, for whom the biographical dictionary became 'a craze', and who spared no expense in sinking funds into the project. Leslie Stephen put into the *DNB* 'more of my life than I quite like'. Unlike its modern counterpart, the *DNB* had no university structure to support it. It was run from offices next door to those of Smith, Elder in Waterloo Place, and linked to them by a speaking tube.

The new *Oxford DNB* has revised and in many cases replaced the old *DNB* articles. The proportion of women included has been dramatically boosted (in a bit of *DNB* ephemera, Brian Harrison informs me that the first woman to infiltrate the hallowed male sanctum of the dictionary was 'a young lady' who arrived in December 1888 'to type manuscripts on an office type-writer that needed some care and attention'). And, in keeping with one of Colin Matthew's earliest editorial decisions, the *DNB* has returned 'to the integrationalist approach of the original edition, in which many minor figures were included, often in half a column . . .'

In 1901, on the completion of the *DNB*, a parody of it was

published entitled *Lives of the 'Lustrious*. Subtitled *A Dictionary of Irrational Biography*, and edited by Sidney Stephen and Leslie Lee, it is full of ingenious skits on the great and the good. As a tribute to one of the dedicatees of *Lives for Sale*, Frances Partridge, who all her life remembered being dandled on Henry James's knee as a child, and to Lyndall Gordon's delightful tale of her amusing experience while writing James's biography, which opens this volume, I would like to end by reprinting the article on James:

James, Henry

Six-shilling sensationalist, was born at Hangman's Gulch, Arizona, in 1843. This favourite author, whose works are famous for their blunt, almost brutal directness of style and naked realism, passed his early years before the mast, and is believed at one period of his career to have sailed under the skull and crossbones. Mr Henry James turned to the pen for a livelihood, and under a variety of pseudonyms produced in rapid succession a large number of exciting stories, the most popular of which are probably *The Master Christian*, *The Red Rat's Daughter*, *The Mystery of a Hansom Cab*, *The Eternal City* and *The Visits of Elizabeth*.

Authorities: Jacobite Papers; Daisy or Maisie or The Two Mad Chicks.

*   *   *

I wish to express my gratitude to Professor Brian Harrison for showing me around the *Oxford Dictionary of National Biography*'s premises at 37A St Giles, Oxford, and for finding the time to talk to me about the history of both the *DNB* and the new dictionary, even as the first volumes of the latter were rolling off the press. I am also deeply indebted to Jean Seaton, widow of Ben Pimlott, who extracted his contribution from his laptop in the weeks immediately following his death in early April 2004. Ben Pimlott was perhaps the finest political biographer of his generation, and his article 'Brushstrokes', published here, is the final piece he ever wrote, while he was in hospital earlier this year undergoing treatment.

At Continuum I would like to thank Andrew Walby and Robin Baird-Smith for their support and advice.

Mark Bostridge
London
May 2004

Lyndall Gordon

The Death Mask

Any biographer who isn't too vain must realize, sooner or later, that what we do is morally indefensible. What Janet Malcolm said of journalists applies equally to our prying and determined curiosity, as we sit in our woollies in properly chilled archives, turning over private letters and diaries. Though I explored the lives of T. S. Eliot and Henry James, writers who took particular pains to resist biography, this issue hardly troubled me until the day I encountered the death mask.

It was June 1997, and the marquee for Commencement was going up in Harvard Yard under the green canopy of the elms. I crossed the campus on my way to the Houghton Library, thinking of Eliot's graduation here in 1910 amid the waving fans of Boston ladies, and his little-known tie with a Bostonian speech teacher who agreed to be cast as his 'Lady of silences'. And going back a further half-century, I pictured Henry James at 20 Quincy Street across the way from the library. In 1867, aged 25, he still lived with his parents and sister, Alice: the protected son, writing his first, civil-war tales about men who find a different kind of heroism from that of fighters. His heroes entered on psychic dramas of withdrawal from brute existence, while his younger brothers, sickly Wilky and wonky Bob, who had fought in the war, were sent out west to be manly in the man-of-action fashion of the age.

It was my last day at the Houghton, a final chance to see the many batches of unpublished James letters, some still wearing their 40-year ban: 'Reserved for Mr Edel' (author of the five-volume biography of James). Now that ban had been lifted, it was possible to search out James's strange, uncategorizable relations with two women: his beloved cousin Minny Temple and 'Fenimore', as he called a reclusive fellow-writer Constance Fenimore Woolson, great-niece of James Fenimore Cooper. These advanced women who died before their time went on to serve as models for portraits of 'Ladies' in James's fiction. I was asking new and, in fact, awkward questions of the manuscripts in the library. Why did James not respond to Minny's dying pleas to be allowed to join him in Europe, as her one chance to 'live'? And why, after Fenimore threw herself out of a window in Venice, did he rush all the way from London to pull out from her papers those that must go in the fire?

There was a succession of fires in James's later life, culminating in a bonfire of letters at his English home in Kent in October 1915, six weeks before the stroke that effectively ended his life. I meant to circumvent that trail of ashes by approaching the private life – the artist's life – through the extraordinary lives and characters of these two women on whom James had fixed his all-seeing eyes. What were they in real life? Were they exalted or thwarted by the purpose of the artist? Sifting through unpublished letters and following clues, I had slowly come to see Minny and Fenimore as biographic subjects in their own right, not passive muses of the Master, for each had been bold enough to cross the boundary of the private life.

I had rather hoped that the claims of the letters would push the death mask off the list, but an hour remained before leaving for the airport. Hardly allowing myself to think, I handed in the request, then went to check the catalogue in an adjoining passage. When I turned back to the reading room, a tall white box waited on the table – so tall that I had to stand to lift the lid. It was like looking down into a grave. I saw a white face, thinner than in life but shockingly lifelike, as though the eyes might open at any moment and look at you. His eyes were what friends had noticed first: light grey and keen (when they were not veiled by his lids), looking at them with scorching intensity as though he could see into their secret selves. The line of his mouth sliced through the lower half of his face, exceptionally wide, parallel to the edge of his eyes. No one saw that mobile mouth in repose. It was always in motion as the Master dictated his works or held forth to admiring listeners, or else pursed those lips in the spectatorial gaze of John Singer Sargent's great portrait of James at 70. That gaze makes the act of looking a Jamesian drama of disconcerting intelligence. He drew friends out in his intent and attaching way; he 'preyed', said Eliot, 'upon living beings', so that the character he came to know was 'the victim of a merciless clairvoyance'.

Eliot's James had been confirmed for me by the experience of the two women who allowed him to know them. They allowed it because they wanted what women want more than anything in the world: to be known for what they feel themselves to be. James was irresistible to women because he met authenticity without fear, a tie in its way more intimate than sex, closer than family or friends. Had Minny and Fenimore understood that intimacy would deepen after their deaths, and that death would release passions impossible in life?

How could a stranger presume to enter into ties more secret than his demonstrative fondness for men? As, transfixed, I stared into that bared face, I felt horribly intrusive. There was no need for James to say, as he does, that one-sided familiarity on the part of the biographer is a 'temptation' to be resisted. For the dead subject has no rights, if his papers be in the public domain, or if his misguided executor authorizes an exhaustive tome – James was scathing about the value of 'quantity'. His sole recourse was to speak through his work, speak as a 'pale, forewarned victim', challenging the conscience of a future intruder. I thought uneasily of his late tale 'The Real Right Thing' where the ghost of a writer appears to a biographer with the deadly name of Withermore, and bars his way.

*   *   *

A little over a year later, I was in a train on my way to give an annual Henry James lecture at the Rye Festival. It was to be an evening event, followed by drinks and dinner in Lamb House, the early Georgian house where James settled exactly a century before, in 1898. A considerate invitation had offered what had been his bedroom for the night.

I had visited Lamb House before, of course, most memorably on an autumn afternoon when a mellow sunlight had burnished the bricks. It had been too late in the year for tourists, and there had been only one other visitor prowling on the other side of a sitting room with glass doors opening on the garden. He said he had directed *Brideshead Revisited* for television, and was now contemplating whether he might have a go at *What Maisie Knew*. Maggie Smith, he thought, would be ideal for the part of the governess who stands by the bereft child of divorced, society parents – James often devised 'situations' that test the moral possibility for innocents to eat of the tree of knowledge and *not* be corrupted.

Now, in September, travelling through Kentish fields, I looked forward to a night in Lamb House with mixed feelings. The public, visiting what is now a National Trust property, is not allowed to wander very far. I'd never seen further than the stair leading upwards from the hall. What lay upstairs? Years of living with James, and concentrating on tales of posthumous encounters (some benign, some not), had alerted me to the insidious atmospheres that inhabit unknown rooms. The death mask was not far from my mind during that journey, nor James's hatred for 'the posthumous exploiter', his shaming phrase for the biographer. I opened the volume of tales I had brought along, and turned the pages to 'The Real Right Thing', published soon after James came to Lamb House. Withermore, his fictional biographer, looks forward at first to 'warm hours with the spirit . . . of his master'. Then, he grows uneasy. 'Great was the art of biography, but there were lives and lives.' Boswell's Johnson was very well, but other lives might 'shrink' in the glare of inspection. The biographic tie offers 'the possibility of an intercourse closer than that of life', yet the closer Withermore comes to his subject – dipping into secrets till he find himself 'face to face' with the dead man – the more he understands what he can't know.

'He strains forward out of his darkness,' Withermore tells the writer's widow; 'he reaches toward us out of his mystery; he makes us dim signs out of his horror . . . He's there to *save* his Life . . . He's there as a curse!'

So, despite his unpromising name, Withermore does do the Right Thing. He gives up as a biographer. Though I had been physically face to face with James, I had not done so.

After the lecture, members of the audience strolled along the cobbled street to Lamb House. There were drinks downstairs. I signed copies of my newly published book, with some relief that nothing had gone wrong. Then it happened. Not upstairs in the dark; not alone in James's room. In the midst of a politely chattering crowd and clinking glasses, in the well-lit hall with its nine-foot door open to the slower steps of aged guests, I felt something slide around my hips. Were ghostly fingers touching me in that close way? As I lifted a glass of wine to my lips in the keen-eyed company of Rye's leading citizens – 'Rye is a hotbed of retired spies,' my host had just informed me, smiling as he sprang that little jolt – my skirt began to slither to the floor.

Backing away from the smile, I clutched Miranda Grant, a

friendly organizer, with my other arm around my collapsing skirt, my most reliable lecture outfit – a black Yamamoto suit from the mid-1980s. Miranda, I could tell, was entertained by a crisis that challenged her considerable flair for order. She raced me upstairs and we fell back laughing on the four-poster. The old, frayed elastic around the waist, we found, had snapped beyond repair. Somehow, Miranda produced a safety pin, and performed some temporary miracle on the now gaping funnel.

'Virginia Woolf once owned to pinning her underwear together with brooches,' she said consolingly.

The absurdity of this scene banished the spectre of Withermore. Coming back to the room, late that night after a fine dinner, I slept deeply. No nocturnal rustle approached the bed; no curse – as far as one can know; only, next day, as I opened my eyes, Miranda Grant, immaculate in jacket and belted slacks, holding out a card of elastic and sitting down to thread her needle. So much for a subtle Jamesian story of ghostly reproach. Instead there was merely a farce of my own making. Another form of justice, you might say.

Andrew Wilson

Personality Rights

I was about as lucky as any biographer can get. Although Patricia Highsmith – best known for her novels *Strangers on a Train* and *The Talented Mr Ripley* – was as secretive and shy as one of the snails which would obsess her throughout her adult life, giving little away to probing journalists, after her death in 1995 her literary estate discovered she had left behind a treasure trove of papers.

From even a cursory glance at Highsmith's archive, it was obvious that this great cache – intimate diaries, notebooks, letters, photographs, sketchbooks – was nothing short of revelatory. I had persuaded her executor to grant me permission to read even the most personal material: diaries which tell of Highsmith's love affairs in astonishing detail. I had started to track down some of the author's friends and lovers. And I had a contract to write her biography.

Then, one day, at the beginning of my research at the Swiss Literary Archives, Berne – the writer spent the last 13 years of her life in Switzerland – I opened the leaf-thin pages of one of her diaries and found something which unsettled me. As I turned to read the scribbles on the inside front cover of her 1942 journal, my eyes focused on a four-line stanza, a poem which cursed anyone who dared peek inside. I paused for a few moments as I felt a rush of blood to my cheeks, feeling as guilty as a character in one of her peculiarly disturbing novels. What should I do? Abandon the project, pay back my advance and risk nothing, or carry on turning the pages to see what kind of secrets they might contain? Of course, in the end the voyeur in me – the voyeur that I suspect lurks in the heart of most biographers – won through. And once I started, I couldn't stop.

In the archive I unearthed the facts surrounding her mother's decision to try to abort Highsmith before she was born. I learnt of the strange, violent dreams that would haunt the writer through-out her life. I read her account of how she thought she was sexually different from an early age – Highsmith singles out the age of 6 as when she first became aware of her lesbianism. From the journals it was obvious that at times she felt near the edge of madness, but somehow she managed to control her dark thoughts and channel them into her writing.

Sex seemed to crop up on every other page of the diaries. Not only did she have intimate relations with dozens of women, but she jumped into bed with her fair share of men, both straight and gay. Yet nothing seemed to satisfy her – she compared sex to a fake Coney Island sideshow, while relations with men she likened to having steel wool rubbed in her face.

As I busily transcribed all this material, together with accounts of her intellectual and creative development, I did not pay much attention to the small print of one of the forms issued by the Swiss Literary Archive at the start of my research. But I was forced to address its implications during the writing of the book. Basically it said that everything held by the archive was covered by a confidentiality clause, thereby pro-tecting the 'personality rights' of everyone named. If I wanted to use anything that was potentially sensitive – in itself a vague, subjective concept – I had to gain permission from each indi-vidual concerned. This was not a case of curatorial obstruction: in fact the staff at the archive were extremely helpful, incredibly insightful and behaved with the utmost professionalism. Rather, it was a formal procedure, a bureaucratic stipulation that covered all their collections.

That, however, did not make it any easier for me. After I questioned the archivists and the estate about this, I was told that not only did I need written consent from those people I had named in the book who were still alive, but those no longer with us. How did they expect me to do that, I wondered? It was simple, came the reply: if a person was dead then I needed to provide them with the written consent of their nearest living relative.

At this point, I seriously considered whether the book that I wanted to write – a frank and honest account of Highsmith's life and work – could ever be published. Before she died, Highsmith had squashed all inquiries from biographers – she likened them to vultures swooping around her – but she was more than happy for her life to be written when she was no longer around to see the result. She also told a friend that her homosexuality should be addressed and that her personal liaisons should be examined. It was for this reason – a sense of personal obligation to her – as well as my own motives (the thought of paying back the advance, not to mention the terrible loss of face) that I persevered.

Over the course of the next couple of months I sent off nearly 100 consent forms, asking people to sign away their 'personality rights' and declare that they were happy to be named in the book. Understandably, such a measure was bound to upset some individuals, but to reassure them that it was nothing more than a formality, I agreed to send back their quotes for approval. 'Did I really say such a thing?' was the most common response. Yes, they did, I gently stated, and it was all captured on tape. Most people were satisfied with merely a minor alteration in punctuation or a quick tidy-up of phrasing or grammar; only one person decided she didn't want her quotes to appear in the book.

One lover, who was married with a child and who refused to co-operate with me from the very beginning, threatened legal action if I so much as hinted at her identity. Yet I felt this woman's role was so key to Highsmith's development (she was, after all, the reason why the writer moved from America to England in 1963) that I wanted to tell the story of their traumatic relationship. After consulting with a lawyer it was decided that this woman would have to be given a *nom de plume*.

The next task was to try to track down the whereabouts of certain lovers named by Highsmith whom I had so far failed to contact. Census records were plundered, old telephone directories raided. After a trawl through public archives I managed to verify the deaths of most of these ex-lovers – those I could not find I described but left unnamed.

I compiled a list for the estate and the curators at the archive outlining the precise status of each individual named, giving the corresponding page number in my manuscript, whether a consent form had been signed, details of death if they were no longer around, and whether they had any offspring. I waited for something like four or five months – a difficult time for me, probably much worse for those around me – until finally I heard that I had been given the go-ahead. Thankfully, as most of the women close to Highsmith did not have children, it was finally decided that, as they were deceased, the risk of legal action was low.

Although the estate and the archive granted me full permission to name the individuals concerned, together with the rights to quote at length from Highsmith's unpublished diaries, notebooks and letters, it has to be said that the research and writing of the biography seemed easy compared with the legal wranglings surrounding it. Despite the fact that Highsmith may have threatened to hex those, like me, who snooped in her diary, I never felt like cursing her. In fact I still feel lucky – and privileged – to have had her as my subject.

Graham Robb

A Narcissist's Wedding

A social worker who becomes romantically involved with a client is likely to be inept. Feelings become confused with needs. Doctors who fall in love with their patients or who find their ailments repulsive should not be trusted. They might become distracted or misinterpret what they hear through the stethoscope. Something similar could be said of any profession. The electrician who came to rewire my house discovered, when he levered up the floorboards, that the house had been insulated by a random but surprisingly large collection of local newspapers dating back to the 1960s. Instead of concentrating on the wiring, he became an enthusiastic amateur researcher and a temporary expert on the early years of Oxford United. As a result, he missed his deadline and may yet be responsible for the incineration of the house and all its contents.

Biography is supposed to be an exception. Biographers are often asked to talk about peripheral or unexpected aspects of their job: the inconvenience of travel, the dustiness of archives and especially their emotional involvement with the subject: How did you feel when they died? (it came as a complete surprise); would you like to have had dinner with them? (hard to answer in the case of Arthur Rimbaud); and even, do you think they would have liked you?

These are certainly important questions. Few books are more tedious than biographies written by people who feel nothing for the subject or, worse, who pretend to have feelings for the subject. Readers are right to be curious. One prolific writer of biographies included in nearly all her introductions phrases such as, 'I have always been fascinated by . . .', suggesting an unusually large repertoire of youthful infatuations. Perhaps there are writers whose biographical vocation reveals itself to them so early that they have time, before leaving school or university, to fall in love with a large enough number of people of sufficient public interest to keep them going until retirement. But they still have to convince the reader of their fascination.

The fantasy of a real relationship with a biographical subject is, at best, a rhetorical device and a marketing ploy; at worst, it turns the biography into a narcissist's wedding.

All this, of course, is a form of self-justification. I never found that my 'relationships' (to speak metaphorically) with Honoré de Balzac, Victor Hugo or Arthur Rimbaud were like relationships with personal acquaintances. I have had more intimate relationships with animals and I might almost say bicycles. I had no responsibility for the happiness of those writers. They neither knew me nor predicted my existence. Arthur Rimbaud died 103 years before I was conceived. Victor Hugo never paid me one of his huge and humbling compliments. Balzac never told me to my face that his *Comédie Humaine* was more real than my own existence. These were not like relationships with living people. My role as a biographer was to tell the truth. No actual relationship could survive, even posthumously, in those conditions.

This detachment – which is not at all the same as emotional neutrality – is the biographer's great advantage. I found it invaluable when writing about Arthur Rimbaud's years in Africa. To judge by the comments of a friend who works with convicted murderers, here was a chance to feel that disgust with the subject which long-distance biographers sometimes experience. Rimbaud gave up writing ('Books are only good for hiding the flaking plaster of old walls') and became a trader on the Abyssinian frontier. In all the biographies and editions I had read, he was presented as a failure. He is said to have lost his money on impractical schemes and to have died a sad but heroic death in the hospital at Marseille. In fact, he made enormous, illegal profits by selling guns to the genocidal King Menelik. Rimbaud had good reasons to present himself as a failure, and never allowed vanity to interfere with business. His competitors, like his biographers, were convinced that the poet 'with soles of wind' was helpless in the real world.

I once spent six weeks with my wife in East Africa (not in Ethiopia and not for the biography), where we lived like impotent gods in a mud hut; I trudged precisely around the town that Rimbaud loathed (Charleville); I even went to Camden Town and Reading. But none of these exercises in distraction and delay could match the discoveries I made in Rimbaud's published correspondence. When Labatut, his gun-running partner, died of throat cancer, the man's widow, an Abyssinian woman, refused to settle her husband's small debts. Since Rimbaud was intending to pocket his partner's share of the proceeds, this was not a serious setback. But, as he told the French Vice-Consul at Aden, he went to the widow's 'shack' and showed how to conduct business on the African frontier:

All I found were some old underpants, which the widow snatched away with tears of fire, a few bullet moulds and a dozen pregnant slaves, which I left . . .

Labatut had been writing his memoirs. I gathered up 34 volumes of them, in 34 notebooks, at the widow's home, and, despite the latter's imprecations, committed them to the flames. This, it was explained to me, was a great misfortune, because some title deeds were interleaved with these confessions which, after a cursory perusal, had seemed to me to be unworthy of serious inspection.

Apart from the grief that it caused, the incineration of the 34 notebooks was also unfortunate because Labatut's memoirs would have been a priceless document on a poorly known period in Abyssinia's history. Labatut died of cancer, but his posthumous existence was snuffed out by Arthur Rimbaud.

Every account of Rimbaud's life either omitted or misrepresented this incident (as well as other such incidents), not because the writers were dishonest but because they had a loving relationship to maintain. Someone they imagined to be Arthur Rimbaud was dictating the tale. My friend who works with murderers was right to be concerned ('How can you spend three years of your life with such a bastard?'). Greed for information dominated everything else. I loved writing the book and I never shed a bitter tear. Remembering what happened to Labatut, I always made several back-up copies of my text and deposited them in different buildings. Call it superstition if you will.

Robert Skidelsky

Confessions of a Long-Distance Biographer

It is no secret that I have spent a large chunk of my life writing about the economist John Maynard Keynes. In 1973, a few months after my son Edward was born, he got a postcard from my mother-in-law. She clearly believed in encouraging early habits of reading. It was of Gwen Raverat's famous watercolour of Keynes as a young man. 'This is a gentleman whom you and Mummy and Daddy will soon grow to hate v. enormously I expect. He looks a bit furtive to me.' My son Edward is now 30.

My original 1970 contract with Macmillan publishers was to write a single-volume 150,000-word biography to be delivered 'not later than 31 December 1972'. This must rank high in the annals of contractual fantasy. The first volume was published in 1983, the second in 1992, and the third in 2000. Recently, the single-volume abridgement was published. As I put it, I hope disarmingly, in its introduction: 'The single-volume life of John Maynard Keynes has been delayed by the publication of my three-volume life.'

I would like to relate some of the highlights of the writing of the life of this remarkable man and to convey something of the flavour of the subject and the challenges of the enterprise. It will be partly at any rate an explanation for my prodigious achievement in tardiness.

The first part of the defence is familiar to most biographers: I could not get access to the necessary papers. Although Sir Geoffrey Keynes, my subject's brother, had given me permission to see the personal papers held at King's College, Cambridge, the economist Richard Kahn, who held copyright of Keynes's economic papers, refused me access. The reason he gave was that a research student of his, Don Moggridge, was editing them for the Royal Economic Society's Collected Edition of Keynes's writings and nothing must be allowed to slow down this valuable project. No less a figure than Harold Macmillan, who had returned to publishing after an interlude as Prime Minister, interceded on my behalf, but to no avail.

Moggridge tried to cheer me up: he would not be long in finishing, and then I would be able to read the material I wanted in the published *Collected Writings*. 'Rest assured,' he wrote to me in July 1970, 'it is not my life's work – not even half a decade's.' However, the volumes of his edition were still being churned out 12 years later, the last one in 1989.

My contract with Macmillan stood, but the completion date was tacitly dropped. Since I was frustrated on the Keynes front, I took a university teaching job in the United States. I returned to an English academic job in 1976, and set about reviving the Keynes project. I would start work on the personal papers and the few already published volumes of the *Collected Writings* and hope that by the time I had finished writing about the early Keynes, the papers of the later Keynes would be open to me.

Only gradually did I realize what a mad undertaking I had let myself in for. The trouble was that Keynes inhabited many different worlds: his curiosities, his sympathies, his ambitions ranged over much of the thought, letters, arts and practical affairs of his time: he even, fortunately briefly, hoped to make a contribution to genetics. He touched almost nothing without leaving a mark on it. How was a biographer to cope? In the introduction to my first volume, I wrote: 'One learns as much as one can in the time available; and for the rest, one hopes, like Bernini, to create an illusion of solidity.'

My serious learning started in the King's College, Cambridge library in 1977. Some diary entries from that summer capture the terror, excitement and pitfalls of research:

12 July: To Hershel Road to see Richard and Anne Keynes. I was dreading it, but they were very friendly, and offered me several large sherries. He suddenly said: 'I want you to see Maynard's letters to Lydia' – so I arranged to start reading them next week.

20 July: Dadie Rylands led me from the library [at King's] to his rooms above it. We sat in his drawing room, full of china, in the window seat where he & Lydia [Lopokova, later Keynes's wife] had acted Comus in 1926. Later saw Simon Keynes at Trinity – an Anglo-Saxon historian, grandson of Geoffrey Keynes and son of Richard and Anne. He let me take away Maynard's Yellow Pedigree Book and his notes. He offered me a huge sherry.

27 July: Drinks with Milo [Richard Keynes's brother] – more sherries – then on to the Arts Theatre for Rattigan's Deep Blue Sea, then back to his house for dinner, to bed at 1.15. The amount of drink one has to go through is simply enormous. He remembers his uncle Maynard coming up to him on his 21st birthday and saying: 'You have now reached the age of copulation.'

Nicky Kaldor, the economist at whose house I was staying, had worked with Keynes as a young man, and he loved discussing (or rather expounding) economics. He was then obsessed by the need to save the world from the evils of 'monetarism', and would develop this theme for hours at a stretch. I would ask questions, which gave him opportunities to lambast Milton Friedman and other assorted 'neo-classical' economists and free-traders. Nicky suffered from narcolepsy, and would often fall asleep in full flow, only to resume 10 or 15 minutes later at exactly the point at which he had left off. He was a wonderful and generous teacher and friend, and I learnt a great deal from these tutorials.

The biographer's most important relationship, apart from that with his or her subject, is with what Virginia Woolf called the 'widow' – the guardian of the Great Man's memory. My two widows were Geoffrey Keynes and Richard Kahn. (Keynes's actual widow, the ballerina Lydia Lopokova, never wanted to talk about her husband and by this time was past talking about anything.) Geoffrey was a brooding presence throughout my early years of research, a powerful force for omission and suppression. He had commissioned Roy Harrod to write the 'official' biography in the late 1940s, and, despite having given me permission to see Maynard's personal papers, saw no need for another life. He was well into his 80s when I started, and his proverbial fierceness had undergone no apparent waning.

Gaining Geoffrey's confidence took several years. Two main problems had to be overcome. The first was that thinking about his brother re-opened too many family wounds. For all his eminence as a surgeon and bibliophile, Geoffrey suffered an acute sense of inferiority in relation to Maynard. He knew that his brother found him a bit of a bore. 'He never liked me when I was young,' he told me. 'It was only when he married Lydia, and she liked me, that he began to think there might be something to me.'

He also resented the fact that his parents had preferred Maynard to him. In their eyes, Maynard was the hare, he was the tortoise; Maynard the charmer, Geoffrey the dry stick. He could hardly bear to talk about his parents, and when he finally wrote his autobiography (published when he was over 90), they got exactly one paragraph.

I used to send him articles I wrote early on about his brother, and he once told me they caused him 'great pain' to read. I was not as tactful as I should have been. I regarded these ephemera as a way of trying out ideas. Geoffrey would treat them as final thoughts, and turn on me. He would withdraw permission for me to see the papers, and the whole relationship would have to be re-established.

The other problem was Maynard Keynes's homosexuality. What purpose did I have, he once asked me, other than to tell the world his brother was a bugger? I replied that it was too late to suppress this, even were it desirable to do so. Michael Holroyd had already revealed most of it in his life of Lytton Strachey; it would surely be far better for Maynard's private life to be placed in the context of his public achievement than for him to be presented as a lecherous appendage to Lytton Strachey. Geoffrey was not convinced. The annoying thing was that whenever the press gave me a 'puff', it was this aspect that they found most titillating for their readers. This confirmed Geoffrey's worst fears.

Gradually things improved, and by the time he died in 1982 we were on excellent terms. The way to Geoffrey's heart was through his library. He had one of the great private collections of antiquarian books, and when I visited him at Lammas House, near Cambridge, we always spent some time looking over them. (One of his favourites was a first edition of Francis Bacon's *Essays*, annotated by William Blake.) As he told me each volume's history, and how he had acquired it, the fierce old man would soften, his face light up in a charming smile. At such moments, one felt he was almost reconciled to the thought of painful revelations in store.

One summer evening he was driven over by his grandson Simon Keynes to have supper with us. I remember Geoffrey almost springing out of Simon's low-slung MG sports car. He must have been 93 by then. His great age made him a figure of awe to our two boys. For some years afterwards, whenever we met anyone who looked moderately old, William would always ask: 'Is he as old as Sir Geoffrey Keynes?'

The keeper of the economic tablets was Richard Kahn, Keynes's 'favourite pupil', who had helped him with the General Theory and lived on at King's College. Kahn was also very old, though not as old as Geoffrey, and, unlike Geoffrey, very deaf. His face was purple, and he had enormous whiskers growing out of his ears, but he had the sweetest of smiles. Now that I no longer badgered him about 'his' papers, he had become very friendly. The truth, which I did not know then, was that he had never liked Roy Harrod's biography of Keynes. But he had his eccentricities. Whenever I appeared at King's, he would greet me warmly and ask me to come and see him 'for a long talk'. 'Only,' he murmured, 'be sure to ring to make an appointment.'

One morning I rang him up. 'Richard Kahn,' said the voice at the other end. I told him who I was. There were some piercing high-pitched whistling noises as his hearing aid was turned on, much audible shuffling of pages (as though of an engagement diary), and an appointment arranged. It had seemed quite easy, and I told Nicky Kaldor that I would shortly be seeing my other widow. Nicky roared with laughter. 'Oh no, you won't. You wait and see.' Early on the morning of the appointed day, the telephone rang. 'This is Richard Kahn. I'm terribly sorry, but I find I have an engagement for this afternoon. Could you come at the same time next week?' This went on for most of one summer and I left Cambridge without our long talk.

When I returned for more research the following year, I ran into Richard by the library steps at King's. 'I think you have been avoiding me,' he said. I did eventually get my interview. It was a grey winter afternoon, and Richard gave me tea in his study above the King's College library. His desk was covered with enormous piles of yellowing paper which, I had no doubt, included several unanswered letters of mine. I was placed in a chair at some distance from him, which did not make conversation easy. As the afternoon wore on, the light faded, but Richard made no move towards the light switch. Eventually we sat facing each other in almost complete darkness. I would shout a question (several times) and finally a ghostly reply would waft towards me through the gloom.

By 1981 I was ready to start writing. Our family decamped to La Garde Freinet in Provence, where we had a house, followed by a van with a huge pile of books. I wrote my first two sentences in September: 'John Maynard Keynes was not just a man of establishments; but part of the elite of each establishment of which he was a member. There was scarcely a time in his life when he did not look down at the rest of England, and much of the world, from a great height.'

La Garde Freinet, a windswept *village perché*, was by no means devoid of intellectual resources. The economist Ian Little had a house just outside the village. Nicky Kaldor had a holiday home. The two economists did not see eye-to-eye, even on matters of theory. Indeed, it was from listening to them argue one lunchtime at Lady Jane Heaton's that I got my great insight that economics was a form of post-Christian theology, with economists as priests of warring sects. Lady Jane lived in some state in a converted chapel in the middle of the village. On either side of her at a long table in the crypt, Kaldor and Little played intellectual tennis of high quality. Nicky served and volleyed with great ferocity, but I noticed that Ian's passing shots were working well. The issue, I remember, was: did Ricardo's theory of comparative advantage assume constant returns to scale? Yes, thundered Kaldor; no, parried Little. Lady Jane presided with a charming but glazed expression, helping them in turns to nourishing soup, which she ladled out from a large tureen.

Halfway through the year, I decided I must learn some mathematics. Few economists in Keynes's day knew much mathematics. Keynes, however, in addition to his other accomplishments, was a Cambridge 'Wrangler' – holder of a First Class honours degree in maths. True enough, by the time he wrote his big books on economics, his mathematics was rusty. My mathematics was not in a position to become rusty: I had retired from the subject at 15 with a rather bad O-level. I did not attribute this poor result to lack of ability, but to poor teaching and lack of motivation. Now I felt I had plenty of motivation. On a visit to London I dropped in at Foyle's and asked for a book on algebra. I returned to our village with *Algebra for Beginners* by Messrs Hall and Knight. This book dated from 1892, which certainly was the right epoch. The algebra Keynes did (at about the age of 8!) I would follow, aged 42, in his footsteps. My wife seemed less than enthusiastic when I suggested we do the examples together, but she warmed noticeably when it became clear that she was consistently getting more right answers than I was. All day I wrote on Keynes at the top of the house; almost every evening from February through till May – when we were not playing Scrabble with Lady Jane – we ploughed through Hall and Knight. As the problems grew more difficult and the evenings longer and warmer, we would take increasingly frequent breaks at the local bar, until one evening we decided we had had enough of algebra.

It was not until November 1982 that I broke the bad news to my agent Michael Sissons: there could be a book in 1983, but it would only be the first of a two-volume set. The reason, I told him, was 'that there is still too much material constantly coming out, which requires mastering and in many cases rewriting of stuff already written'.

Although my schedule had always been fanciful, this was true. It turned out that the 'economic papers', to which I finally gained access that autumn, contained masses of unpublished philosophical manuscripts. Reading them for the first time not only caused me to rewrite (in a great hurry) a fundamental chapter in my first volume, but also sharpened my intuition that there were important connections to be made between Keynes's theories of ethics and probability, and his economics – connections which had to do with the problem of rational behaviour under conditions of uncertainty. However, it was also true that the scale on which I was writing the life was totally inconsistent with a one-volume treatment.

The first volume was published to what are called 'glowing' reviews. What I felt I had succeeded in doing was rescuing the young Keynes from the 'moist light' with which Roy Harrod, according to Noel Annan – reviewing the Harrod book – had irradiated him. I was particularly pleased to get the following from Richard Kahn: 'I found [your book] most impressive, interesting and beautifully written. You have taken enormous trouble, covering a much wider field than might have been expected – I look forward to the further volumes.'

My relationship with Kahn had, as this letter suggests, now entered a benign period. Richard was at Nicky Kaldor's funeral in the autumn of 1986. At drinks afterwards, he was sitting alone in the dining room, by the sideboard, isolated from the throng by his deafness, age and temperament. It was the last time I saw him. He died a few months later. At the end he suffered from delusions. One evening, so I heard, he rang the porter at King's College. When the porter appeared, Richard pointed to a large cupboard in the corner of his study. 'Nicky Kaldor is on top of that,' he said in a quiet voice. 'Would you please ask him to leave?'

By this time I had decided that there must be three volumes, since in my first I had only got Keynes up to 1919, or age 36, and barely started on his economics. Barring the way stood the 'Keynesian Revolution', hardly an under-excavated topic. Thousands of articles and books had appeared analysing what Keynes had said, what he was meant to have said, what he should have said, what others said he had said, etc. Where, amid all this exegesis, did my comparative advantage lie? What value could I add?

Here begins the second round of my defence. As I got deeper into my work I became obsessed with two questions: how does a historian write about an economist? And what is the value of biography? Over the period I was writing about Keynes, many of the old conventions were breaking down. Historians' range was increasing as they were becoming better trained technically. Biographies were becoming franker, and biographers were becoming more self-conscious about their craft.

The answer to the first question was obvious: learn economics. I am amazed this had not occurred to me before I embarked on the project. I had picked up some economics while working on my first book, *Politicians and the Slump*, an account of the Great Depression of 1929–31. My real economic education started with my 'tutorials' with Nicky Kaldor in the late 1970s. But reading Keynes himself was the greatest of all lessons in economics, especially for its revelation of how an economist's mind works. I was convinced that any account of Keynes which failed to engage with his 'theology' would be seriously incomplete as history.

But in learning economics it was equally important, I felt, not to lose one's historical bearings, the sense that economic doctrines are heavily contextual, and that biography is above all about character and context, not about propositions. Even though there is a logical core to all economic thinking, a biographer of

Keynes, nevertheless, always had to keep in his mind the question of why Keynes's doctrines were developed at that particular time and why they succeeded in the world of action, while those of his opponents failed. These are historical, not economic, questions. My own biographical enterprise spanned exactly the years when Keynesian economics was fading, and when it started to be possible for Keynes to be seen as a historical figure – as an exemplar and product of the problems, virtues and defects of his age. Knowledge of economics is necessary to understand Keynes's 'theology'; a strong historical sense is necessary to maintain the necessary detachment from the theology. Today I would describe myself not as an economist but as an economically literate historian.

The second volume of the trilogy was published in 1992. I had got Keynes through his great book, *The General Theory of Employment, Interest and Money*, published in 1936. I now think there was too much economics in this volume, so keen was I to show that I could 'do' it. What Keynes demonstrated – what he is famous for – is that employment could be limited by lack of effective demand. This overturned the 'classical' view that the amount of employment depended on individual choices for work or leisure. This implied that all unemployment was in some sense voluntary, as it undoubtedly was for that small class of persons who used to be called the 'idle rich'. But to use this kind of model to explain why millions of workers suddenly found themselves out of work was absurd. Only an economics long since detached from common sense could view the Great Depression from this standpoint. Today it is generally accepted that unemployment can occur for 'Keynesian' reasons, though what can cause demand to be deficient is hotly disputed between rival sects of economists. In one very important sense, Keynes has 'won' the argument, despite all Thatcherite backslidings. There are Keynesian economists and non-Keynesian economists, but no pre-Keynesian economists. And the same goes for governments.

With Volume 2 published, there were nine years only of Keynes's life to go, though these covered the years of his greatest public activity, during and immediately after the Second World War, and included his greatest practical achievement, the Bretton Woods Agreement of 1944. But Volume 3 was published only in 2000. For this last gap between the volumes there is no defence, only explanation.

Most of the 1990s were taken up with other activities. In 1991 I was made a life peer and became chairman of the Social Market Foundation. In 1994 I made my first trip to post-communist Russia and spent a year writing a short book, *The World After Communism*. From 1992 to 2001 I took the Conservative whip in the Lords, before joining the cross benches. However, I played my political cards in such a cunning way that I was able to resign or get dismissed from all the political jobs to which I was appointed, which in due course precluded further offers. Thus the road to Keynes's death was kept open.

Along that road I had been wrestling with a dense thicket of problems peculiar to biography. The chief of these were: what is the relationship between a thinker's life and his thought? And what difference do individuals make?

In his obituary of Keynes, the Austrian economist Joseph Schumpeter had written: 'He was childless and his philosophy of life was essentially a short-run philosophy.' My account of Keynes's homosexuality gave critics of Keynesian economics their chance. William Rees-Mogg argued in *The Times* in 1983 that Keynes's rejection of moral rules led him to reject the gold standard which provided an 'automatic control of monetary inflation'. Admirers of Keynesian economics moved, with a kind of reflex action, to insulate the 'thought' from the 'life'. Thus

Maurice Peston wrote in the *New Statesman* in 1983 that 'it is obvious philosophical nonsense to suggest that there is a connection [between Keynes's sexuality and his economics]; the logical validity of a theory and its empirical relevance are independent of its progenitor. (What help is knowledge of the lives of Newton and Einstein in predicting the movements of the planets?)' Rees-Mogg and Peston, it seems to me, were guilty of opposite errors. The riposte to Rees-Mogg is that a correlation is not a cause, and to Peston that economics is not a science like physics.

The most powerful theory of the connection between life and work is Freud's, and Freud's theory of the mind has spawned a great many biographies of uneven quality. I have a temperamental antipathy to Freudian explanations of 'achievement'. It seems to me that they are incurably reductionist. They give the biographer warrant to treat the psychological provenance of an idea more seriously than the idea itself. In any event, I found the Freudian approach unhelpful in writing about Keynes. The specific psychological mechanism used by Freud to explain rebellion – the Oedipal Complex – seemed irrelevant in Keynes's case, either as an explanation of Keynes's homosexuality, or of his revolutionary economics. He was a rebel against Victorian orthodoxies, but this was not a revolt against his father, or his family's values. Sociology offered a better clue. The idea of Keynes as an Edwardian, who tried, by manipulating economic facts, to restore a post-Victorian sense of security after the horrors of the First World War, seemed to me, as it still does, a better biographical setting for Keynes's economics than any circumstances of his childhood.

I am more sympathetic to Freud's poetry than to his psychology. He had a tragic vision of life, and saw the suppression of the instinctual desires as the price of civilization and progress. It is possible to write about Keynes in this way: duty triumphed over inclination, Bloomsbury was sacrificed to Whitehall. But even this is to get things off-beam. One has no sense of a tragic life, but of a happy, successful and fulfilled one. He succeeded in getting the best of all his possible worlds. It is significant that Freud, with his wealth of classical stereotypes, never discussed Odysseus, the classical hero 'soft of speech, keen of wit, and prudent', whom Keynes most resembled.

I have some sympathy for the neo-Marxist view that Keynes was a product of his class and background, who tended to see the economic problem from the standpoint of the 'educated bour- geoisie' located at the centre of a declining empire. One can add a great deal of sophistication to this kind of approach. But it does not absolve the biographer from taking Keynes's ideas seriously, and leaves out the value added by genius, that residual of universal significance.

A work of genius is a complex subject, and there is light to be shed about what went into the making of it. Even in the case of scientific and mathematical achievement we can say a great deal about the intellectual background from which it was fashioned: the existing state of knowledge, the puzzles left unsolved by the orthodoxy of the day, why those puzzles were, or had become, interesting, the particular capacities which the solver brought to their solution. At the other extreme is a work of art which seems to have much more immediate roots in the personal life of the artist or writer. In between is the area in which Keynes worked, which was partly scientific, partly artistic. This gives a wide justification for a biographical approach. As I put it in the introduction to my first volume: 'If underlying Keynesian theory was Keynes' vision of his age, knowledge of his state of mind and the circumstances which formed it is essential, not only in order to understand how he came to see the world as he did, but also in order to pass judgment on the theory itself.'

This said, I do not want to argue the case for biography on utilitarian grounds. People do, of course, read biography partly to understand what formed the character and work of an outstanding person. But they also read it because it is the oldest form of story-telling, which long antecedes fiction. We want to know, and seem always to have wanted to know, how famous people lived their lives, and to hear the stories of their exploits and the great events in which they were involved. There is no dimunition of this interest, which is why biography remains one of the most popular reading genres.

What, finally, is biography's relation to history? The famous lines from Ecclesiasticus, which start: 'Let us now praise famous men', were read at Keynes's memorial service in Westminster Abbey in 1946, and it is in these terms that I have finally come to see him. This is a Great Person view of history. But this is my belief. Individuals do make a difference; Keynes made a difference. No doubt, all the separate influences are absorbed in the long course of history. But I doubt if any serious historian today would deny that great men and women are one of these 'separate influences'. This is the justification for writing about them.

'But, soon or late, it is ideas, not vested interests, which are dangerous for good or ill', Keynes wrote, in one of his most famous passages. I have often puzzled about the word 'dangerous'. Keynes was a most careful user of words. How can ideas be dangerous for good? A more obvious word would be 'powerful'; the thought behind it being that ideas have a stronger influence on events, for good or bad, than have interests. And this is how the passage is usually interpreted. But the word 'dangerous' adds a subtlety characteristic of Keynes: the thought that ignorance is dangerous, but that knowledge, too, is dangerous, because it tempts to hubris – the usurpation by humans of divine powers – whose inevitable fruit is nemesis. That Keynes's great revolutionary manifesto, *The General Theory of Employment, Interest and Money*, should have ended on this oblique note of warning is striking testimony to a greatness that transcended economics. An intellect that could soar, seemingly without limit, accepted the discipline of earth-bound limits in the management of human affairs. This is the Keynes I love, and whose personality and achievements I have tried to convey.

Hermione Lee

A Great House Full of Rooms

1. At The Mount

I am writing a life of Edith Wharton, the great American novelist who lived from 1862 to 1937. This work has involved me in some wonderful journeys, because as well as writing 45 books, Wharton was also a traveller, a wartime administrator, a house designer and a gardener. She thought architecturally – in an early story she says 'a woman's nature is like a great house full of rooms' – and to visit her houses is also to understand her character and her way of life. The first two houses she decorated, soon after her unfortunate marriage to Teddy Wharton, were in Newport, Rhode Island, but her third house, which she had designed and built, was The Mount, built on a hillside in Lenox, Massachusetts between 1901 and 1902. Her friend Henry James called it a 'delicate French chateau mirrored in a Massachusetts pond'. It was certainly designed – by the architect Francis Hoppin, with some indoor help from Ogden Codman – with Europe in mind. You can see reflected in it the principles of design which she had expressed in her first book, co-authored with Codman in 1897, *The Decoration of Houses*. She wanted to import European style to American house design, but not in a superficial or flashy way. The Mount cost about $80,000 all told, but that was much less than some of the other grandiose millionaires' 'cottages' in Lenox.

The design is 'simple and architectural', showing proportion and balance: it is like her prose style. It's a big white H-shaped house with a huge terrace running along the length of the first floor, with French windows opening on to the terrace and a Palladian flight of steps down to the gardens. The house and gardens have been newly restored by the Edith Wharton Restoration Society. Photographs show that the gardens were very much in the Italian style, with a secret sunken walled garden with statues, a linden walk, a rock garden, parterres and flower gardens. The house has 35 rooms and 100 windows (some of them false), all with green shutters. It looks spacious, confident, rather masterful. Inside, it is all about privacy, efficiency, comfort and order. The main stairs are hidden away behind a glass door to the side of the grotto-like entrance hall. The first-floor rooms open off a long Italianate gallery. The library is a model of luxurious unpretentiousness. On the second floor, Edith had her own little suite: the bedroom where she wrote, her own bathroom and boudoir (where she answered her letters). Every detail has been thought through, from the mother-of-pearl bell-pushes to the heart-shaped hooks in the guest bedrooms. This is a way of life based on live-in servants (ten in the house, ten in the grounds), who have their own staircase and their own attic floor. It's also a house made for work and entertaining. I could imagine Henry James reading Whitman aloud in front of the library fire, and setting off on jaunts in the new car.

One of the interests that drew Henry James and Wharton together was their fascination for George Sand. When I went to visit George Sand's house at Nohant, as they did on their 'motor flight' through France in 1907, I was struck by differences and similarities. Nohant is a solid, modest, elegant French provincial bourgeois manor house, not at all grand, deeply entrenched in its traditions and history. The village lies around the house, the little church stands just outside the gates of the house. George Sand grew up there – it was her grandmother's house – and lived there for much of her adult life. She was rooted in the place and the landscape. Nothing could be more different than Wharton's imposition of a massive European house onto a Massachusetts landscape, or than the few, increasingly unhappy, years she spent there, interspersed with long stays in Italy and France. (It was sold in 1911 because of the breakdown of the marriage.) Yet the life Wharton created at The Mount was not entirely unlike George Sand's life at Nohant. Both were domestic women, good housekeepers, who gave energetic and scrupulous attention to their houses and gardens, while keeping up unostentatious, private, efficiently time-tabled lives as professional writers. Both made their houses into welcoming havens for visiting writers. And both used their surroundings for some of their best fictional work.

Wharton's stories of women living in such New England homes are lonely, chilling, haunted tales. But she was also inspired by the countryside around, its mountainous beauty, its extremes of wealth and rural poverty and small-town industrial hardship. It is out of towns like Pittsfield and North Adams – which still show the legacy of hard New England poverty – that she wrote *Ethan Frome, The Fruit of the Tree* and *Summer.*

While I was in Lenox I went on a picnic – Edith was very good at organizing picnics – to a landmark she knew well, a little hill with wooded slopes called Tyringham Cobble (she wrote a poem about that hill). It's a steep climb up from fields through shady woods and out onto rocks and high, rough meadows. Up there, leaning against a maple tree, looking down towards the valley in hot July sunshine surrounded by birdsong and butterflies and the odd snake, I thought about her grand, luxurious house, and the contrast between that and her simple, passionate love of this American countryside which, at 50, she would leave and never see again.

2. In Italy

Between 1885 and 1905 – the 20 years during which Edith Wharton transformed herself from Newport hostess to best-selling author of *The House of Mirth* – she spent much of every year in Italy. Later, from about 1911, she became great friends with the art historian Bernard Berenson, and often visited him at I Tatti, his villa outside Florence. She immersed herself in Italian history, architecture, art and literature. She was eager to be a pro-fessional connoisseur, not just an enthusiastic tourist. She wrote three books about Italy (two about places and villa-gardens, and an eighteenth-century historical novel). Though she is more often associated with America and France, Italy was one of the great passions of her life. Most of her Italian travelling was before her love affair with the motor car became possible, but she was an intrepid and determined traveller by train, donkey cart, mule, funicular, or whatever would get her to an out-of-the-way shrine, monastery or ruin.

I have been following in her footsteps to some of the northern Italian cities she writes about so well in *Italian Backgrounds* (1905) – Mantua, Parma, Padua, strange little Sabbioneta, Milan – and to some of the villas she describes in *Italian Villas and Their Gardens* (1904). Whenever I set a place against her description of it, I see how brilliantly focused and judicious she is. Take, for instance, her favourite place in Milan, the little fifteenth-century chapel, the Portinari chapel, in a church called Sant'Eustorgio. It is a dazzling mix of terracotta decorations and delicate frescoes, with a frieze of terracotta angels swinging big bells of fruit and flowers, all around the round ceiling. Wharton describes it per-fectly as 'a masterpiece of collaboration between architect and painter', and says, quite rightly, that the whole chapel has a mood of 'blitheness'. And so it does.

Following her lead, we took the boat called the *burchiello* along the Brenta canal from Padua to Venice, to look at the Palladian villas, pleasure houses built for the Venetian gentry, which she describes so eloquently. She imagines the days of hedonistic carefree life in places like the great Villa Pisani at Stra, and calls up the melancholy sense of the vanished past that hangs over a sombre villa like the Malcontenta. And always, Wharton gets the tone of the place exactly right, through her close reading of details and through paying attention to the way these buildings were used and to the historical transitions they display.

Sitting in the garden of one of the most magical of the Tuscan villas she describes, the Villa Gamberaia at Settignano, outside Florence, in June, listening to the cuckoos calling from the olive groves and the frogs croaking in the lily pond, looking down at the Arno valley through the sculptured yew hedges, and wandering about its water-parterres, its long green bowling alley, its secret grotto-fountain and sunken garden, its terrace with lemon trees in their pots, its little dark woods and its terrace with stone dogs, I could see exactly what Wharton means by the combination of 'logic and beauty' in the best Italian garden design. The garden is an extension of the house and is made to connect to the landscape, and it works through contrasts and variety and what she calls 'breadth and simplicity of composition'. That's what influenced her building of The Mount; and that's what she wants in her writing of fiction.

3. At the Pavillon

Wharton lived in France from the age of 50 until her death at 75. After her Paris years before and during the war, her French residences were seasonal. Just after the war, she took over, and did up, two French houses and gardens. One is in Hyères, east of

Toulon, a house called Château Sainte-Claire, on a hillside above the little town, in the grounds of a ruined seventeenth-century convent, with a staggering view down to the Mediterranean, where she spent the winters. The other is on the outskirts of Paris, in a small town called Saint-Brice-sous-Fôret, on the edge of the Montmorency Forest, a long, low, eighteenth-century house called 'Pavillon Colombe', named after the two Venetian actresses for whom it had been built. This is where she spent her summers. She designed two magnificent – and quite different – gardens for these houses. One was a hillside Mediterranean garden of a series of sloping terraces connected by little paths, cypress arches and stone walls, lavish with roses, exotic shrubs like bougainvillea and mimosa, succulents, and massed drifts of intensely coloured flowers. The other was an enclosed northern garden with a terrace, geometric parterres divided by box hedges, a pond with a fountain, a wood, a kitchen garden, and small gardens like little rooms where different palettes of colours predominated, like her blue garden. Both still exist, and show the traces of Wharton's gardening.

After battling through the Paris suburbs to the now rather dingy Saint-Brice, and after some prolonged courting of the princess who owns the Pavillon, I finally pay my visit to Wharton's house. The butler, complete with gloves and uniform, leads us into the central reception room, done up in Chinoiserie style. The princess, who is upset today by the death of her borzoi, but is extremely hospitable, tells us that the house was largely redesigned by its next owner, the Duchesse de Talleyrand, and by herself: indeed, she doesn't seem to think much of Edith's taste in furniture. But the garden is being tenderly kept up, and she lets me go up to the bedroom where Wharton died, with the pond outside one window, where she used to feed the fish, with the scents and sounds of the garden coming up through the front windows. Some things have had to go: the princess tells me that, unlike Edith, she hates white dahlias, but, wanting to be faithful to her great predecessor, has obtained satisfactory replacements. Sure enough, out on the terrace, there are two rather shame-faced looking white peacocks, pretending to be dahlias.

Frances Wilson

A Love Triangle

The true horror of what follows cannot be appreciated unless it is understood that all biographers live in fear of sharing their subject with a third party. The announcement of a biographer working on the same person as ourselves is worse than the interruption of a wedding by the appearance of a previously unheard-of spouse; worse than the rival appearing on the honeymoon and demanding conjugal rights. It beats any other form of cuckoldry or infidelity because the feelings a biographer holds towards his or her subject put the regular sentiments entertained by romantic love in the shade. Biographical love is uxorious on a Grand Scale. It is obsessive, possessive, irrational and perverse passion of a kind that the rest of us rarely feel towards anyone we have actually *met* or might claim to really *know*. The biographer venerates the very shoelaces their subject wore, and fetishizes their every laundry bill. Months are spent in pursuit of the same views, the same walks, the same weather, the same spartan journeys across land and sea. The biographer knows the facts of the subject's life far better than those of his or her own family. But having said that, part of the madness of biographical love is that most biographers find it hard to distinguish themselves from their subjects anyway.

Just as few can love with quite the same fervour as the biographer-at-work, so few can hate with the same mouth-foaming, vitriolic venom as when their subject is spreading his or her pleasures abroad. Otherwise quiet and reasonable bookish-types, confronted by the sharing of a local county archive with the Rival, entertain fantasies of poison gas and hit-men. Every biographer has a tale to tell about being haunted by a rival. But if one rival gives the effect a turn of the screw, what do you say to *two* rivals?

Which preamble brings me to the events of summer, 2003. I had completed my life of the Regency courtesan, Harriette Wilson. As her first proper biographer, I felt as though I had taken her virginity. Not many had heard of her, so she was all mine. The letters I found had not been read before, her blackmailing of the king had not previously been known. She and I had a special relationship. It was three months before we were going public as a couple and I went to see my editor to discuss the proofs. He looked ashen. I had a Rival, it seems, who had, unknown to us, been lurking there all along. Her book even had the same title as mine. A chill went down my spine. Fool that I was! Of course such happiness could not have been real. I was a gull, a pur-blind cuckold. Harriette's and my relationship had been a mockery, we would never be glued to one another for posterity, like Boswell and Johnson or Froude and Carlyle. Instead we would be memorialized in a love-triangle with the Rival. Our books would appear together, be reviewed together, be stocked on the shelves together. Readers would have to choose between them.

While my editor discussed trivia such as title changes and promotional tours, I sat gazing into a black and midnight pit, a cavernous realm of my psyche I had until now been unaware of. From the perspective of the pit, my relationship with Harriette Wilson seemed rather different from the scholarly one I had until now assumed we enjoyed. My investment in Harriette, apparently, bore no relation to intellectual engagement, no relation to myself as an academic or a writer. Gone was any pretence that I had written an objective life of a historically important figure: Harriette Wilson and I were co-dependent, we were in it together, we gave each other substance, we could not be separated without losing oxygen. *She could not be in a relationship with someone else at the same time because it stripped me of identity.* It wasn't the sharing of publicity about to take place which left me choking for air, but the sharing of Harriette's person which had *already taken place.* Had our intimacy been nothing but a fantasy?

The two books appeared and Harriette and I parted ways. A biographer on a rebound, I was on the look-out for a new subject. I cruised through libraries in my desparate state, preparing to take on anyone who was currently unattached. Arthur Conan Doyle, Bram Stoker, Richard Brinsley Sheridan . . . men seemed a safer bet than women. I tried them all out but was not sufficiently attracted. The feelings would no doubt grow, but I wanted it to be love at first sight.

And then, after months of searching, I met someone. She was ideal: the right age, the right interests, the right background; here was someone I could communicate with. She was another early nineteenth-century Londoner who had been forgotten, a poet whose life suited my interests; the perfect person with whom to get over Harriette. Like Harriette, this woman was transgressive and marginal. She lived in a twilight world. She was, like Harriette, adored by the public and then discarded; her life was full of secrets, her public persona bore no relation to the private person whose mysterious death in Africa was still not explained. She was also virgin territory; there was an untold story to uncover here. I felt completed. I was ready to get involved again, to follow the trail she had left, to think with her thoughts. I told my editor about my new relationship. It was agreed that we were a good couple, that we could go a long way together.

And then the bombshell. Someone else, I heard, was *interested in the poet.* They had been *obsessed with her for years,* far longer than me. I was the Rival, the cuckolder, the destroyer of relationships. The Other Biographer had, as yet, no book contract, but my new subject was nonetheless spoken for. So what? Friends said, why let that stop you? There is room for two books. Good point, I thought, I'll just push on with it. Then the letter came. The Other Biographer had heard about me and wrote to warn me off; she would beat me to the post, she said; she knew about things I could never discover, she knew the poet's family, they were co-operating with her. She pleaded with me as a woman, as a mother; there were others I could write about, and she suggested some names. Her husband had been out of work, she was resting her own career on this biography, she asked me not to ruin her life. She knew my writing, she said, and was convinced that my representation of the poet would be the same as hers, that there would not be room for both of us. She was writing to me from the heart of the black and midnight pit, into whose cavernous realms I too was once again gazing. *I too could not share the poet with a third party.* I too wanted the peace of a monogamous relationship. I did not want, every time I read her poems, to think about the Other Biographer. But I wanted to have a part of the poet. I became obsessed, not with the poet but with the O.B. Soon the O.B. and the poet merged into one person. Should I continue with the biography or not? Could I write under these conditions? I put all my books by and about her into boxes and hid them under a cloth. I was not going on, I told my editor; I felt sick at the thought of continuing. Rubbish, everyone said. Out came the books once more. I sat at my desk. I couldn't open them. Soon I couldn't go into my study at all because The Books were in there. My study became the black and midnight pit. Back in the boxes The Books went, then out again, then in, then out. Like the ancient mariner I cornered people and told them my woeful tale. Get on with it, they said, eyes glazing over with boredom. Write your blessed book.

A trip had been booked to Africa, where the poet had died. I had to go or the ticket would be wasted. Off I went, to a country

I disliked, to research a woman about whom I now had a phobia. Visiting her grave every day, I felt I could continue with the research and I even managed to draft a first sentence. But home again, faced with The Books in the study, I froze. Back they went into the box. In the autumn I was in the British Library when a woman approached me. She looked tired, her voice was soft, she was about my age. Was I Frances Wilson, she asked? I started to shake, violently. My throat went dry. I knew it was the O.B. I could hear, above the thunderous noise in my ears, that we were chatting about our journeys to the library and how hard they were to make with young children at school. Then she asked me about my biography: was I continuing with it? No, I said. Well, yes. Yes and no. I didn't know. I was interested in it but in a different way from her. I wanted to write on the poet but I didn't know quite how I was going to do it. I wouldn't steal her thunder, I assured her, using a term she had used in her letter. I might just write about the end of the poet's life. I would keep her informed with what I was doing. She looked visibly relieved. My heart lightened at her relief. Something extraordinary had happened. *I liked the Other Biographer.* I not only sympathized with her: I *liked* her. To tell the truth, I told her, the poet's interminable depression and total lack of humour wore me down. I couldn't stand her company for long.

I went home and The Books came out of the boxes. I told my editor and agent that I had met the O.B. and felt free now to begin my work. Differently. But I had another book to write first. On something even stranger than my poet and her death, and on an area even more virginal: the perverse, irrational, quite marvellous relationship between biographers and their subjects.

Jeremy Lewis

Pantherine

I have mixed feelings about biographies in general, and literary biographies in particular. I don't want to read the wretched things, and a large part of me rather despises the whole business as second-hand and second-rate, yet I've enjoyed my belated career as a biographer more than anything else I've done in my professional life (apart, that is, from helping out at the *London Magazine* and *The Oldie*). A passionate devotee of memoirs and autobiographies, I regard biography as the most ephemeral of all literary forms, with Boswell and Lytton Strachey the exceptions that prove the rule; yet despite the mediocrity of most practitioners, and the ludicrous claims made on its behalf, I harbour the hope that, in theory at least, the detailed and sympathetic recreation of someone else's life – poignant and funny all at once, and vividly populated with subsidiary characters – could be worthy to stand alongside the great Victorian novelists: it attempts, after all, the resurrection of the dead, and what could be more miraculous than that?

I began my reluctant career as a biographer in 1992, when – for no very obvious reason – I was commissioned to write the authorized biography of Cyril Connolly. Early on in the proceedings, a helpful and experienced biographer friend drew me aside and pointed out that, since many of Connolly's surviving friends and contemporaries were, by then, in their 80s and 90s, I should hurry off at once and interview them before it was too late. Dutiful as ever, I plodded off to see assorted octogenarians, but soon realized that I had been offered dud advice: I knew far too little about Connolly to ask the right questions, while they – very understandably – recycled the same old stories from memoirs of their own; and I realized very quickly that memory was a fallible affair, and that even the most well disposed were prone to both amnesia and flights of fancy. After a month or so, I decided to call a halt *pro tem*. I would go away and do my homework, returning to the fray after immersing myself in primary and secondary sources, and if some survivors had popped off in the meantime, that was a risk worth taking: all the more so since I soon realized that although I was perfectly happy to be a voyeur at one remove, riffling greedily through the most intimate letters and diaries, I was far more craven and constrained when faced with flesh and blood, feeling myself to be an uneasy cross between a Peeping Tom and a double-glazing salesman.

Among those I would have to beard sooner or later was Cyril Connolly's second wife, Barbara Skelton, a notorious *femme fatale* to whom the adjective 'pantherine' was invariably attached. She had been married to Cyril Connolly, George Weidenfeld and Derek Jackson, the millionaire Oxford don and amateur jockey whose family had owned the *News of the World*; her lovers had included King Farouk (who beat her with his dressing-gown cord), Felix Topolski, Peter Quennell, Alan Ross (with whom I was then working on the *London Magazine*), Kenneth Tynan and the cartoonist Charles Addams. All this was daunting enough; and her alarming reputation appeared to be borne out by her memoirs, comical and bitchy in equal measure, and by her tawny-haired, high-cheeked, almond-eyed good looks, like a ferocious ice maiden painted by Cranach. She was then living in France, so, with Alan Ross's encouragement, I dropped her a line and asked if we could meet. We did so in London, and I was much taken with her silvery laugh, her innate good sense on literary matters, her slim but voluptuous figure (she must have been in her mid-70s, but her allure was as potent as ever), and the snorts of derision with which she dismissed so many of those she had known in that seductive, raffish world where Bohemia and Society intersect. Connolly, as I soon discovered, had been the love of her life, and although she keenly ridiculed his foibles, she always spoke of him with affection and admiration.

Back in France, she urged me to come and stay in her cottage south of Paris. She told me that I must on no account allow her 'pussers' (a pair of bad-tempered Burmese cats) to escape into the garden; we drank a great deal, and I noticed how, when standing in the kitchen, she endlessly wiped immaculate surfaces with a wad of kitchen paper. She didn't seem particularly interested in discussing her life with Connolly; but then, as if opening a treasure chest, she suddenly showed me a window seat crammed with Sainsbury's shopping-bags, each of them bulging over with his letters, hurled in higgledy-piggledy, with or without envelopes attached. 'I *might* – just might – let you look at these one day,' she said, in her taunting, half-teasing way; and with that she closed the window seat, and turned to other matters.

Later that summer, she decided to move back to England: she was lonely in France, she hated the 'Frogs', and life might be better on the other side of the Channel. One day she rang and asked if I would do her a great favour: would I come over to Paris, where she had a flat, help her to pack up, and drive her and the pussers back to London, where she had taken a flat off the King's Road? Flattered to be asked, and happy to escape from my desk, I jumped on a bus and headed towards the Calais ferry. Barbara was in a filthy mood when I arrived – clad in a dressing gown, hemmed in by crates, clutching a brimming glass of whisky, and emanating ill humour. In due course I learned that the only antidote to her sulks was to make her laugh, so triggering the silvery laugh: as it was, she smouldered noisily while I cleared the flat and then, awash with whisky, we loaded the back of her Renault Clio with dresses, boots, boxes, the pussers in their cage, quarantine-bound, books galore, a Toulouse Lautrec drawing and, teetering uneasily on top of it all, a Sidney Nolan painting of a lugubrious-looking water-fowl picking its way through a swamp. Kitted out with a pair of string driving-gloves, Barbara took the wheel, but after shooting past the Calais exit on the Peripherique and attempting a U-turn in a motorway maintenance area filled with gravel, she ordered me to take the wheel. As we sped in a northerly direction, she refreshed herself from the whisky bottle and barked out commands to drive 'Faster, faster'.

Back in London, high up in a hideous tower block at the bottom end of Sydney Street, she found herself even lonelier than in France. Over the years she had managed to offend many of her old acquaintances, and those who had not taken umbrage were, more often than not, no longer around to help drain the whisky bottle. Petra and I soon found we had become extremely fond of Barbara, albeit in the nervous, uneasy way in which one might become fond of some beautiful undomesticated animal that was liable to whip out its claws at any moment. We were also all too well aware that if we didn't bother with her, then few others would: a duty we shared with a handful of far older friends like Alan Ross, Jocelyn Rickards and Clive Donner, Carol Topolski, Cressida Connolly and her husband Charles, and the arch-gossip Ali Forbes. 'Well, *you're* not much of a friend, are you?' she'd say if I failed to ring every other day at least; she remained as flirtatious and as seemingly seductive as ever, but if I gave her so much as a formal peck on the cheek she went quite rigid, as if she'd been plugged into the mains. One day, greatly daring, I raised the matter of my trawling through the letters in the polythene bags. She brooded for a while before coming up with a solution satisfactory to us both. She had never been able to read

Connolly's handwriting: she would allow me to read his letters on the condition that I typed them out at the same time; that way we could both enjoy them. It seemed a dotty idea – there were hundreds of letters, jumbled together and hopelessly out of order, and matters were made worse by Connolly's refusal to date his letters – but I could think of no alternative. Barbara lent me her old portable, stretched herself out on the bed, and, using her dressing-table as a desk, I began to work my way through the mound. Barbara soon became bored by the proceedings. '*Now* what's Cyril saying?' she would ask; I would read out bits from the letter in question, Barbara would give a shriek of mirth ('So *that's* what he was up to!') and, with luck, place the letter in some kind of context. But it was, I knew, a doomed venture: after a week's typing, endlessly interrupted, I had barely made an impression on the great wodge of sky-blue airmail letters. At this rate, I would spend the next ten years at least working on my biography; some other way round would have to be found.

While all this was going on, Barbara had decided that she needed a country cottage as well as a flat in London, ideally not too far from Cressida Connolly's house in Worcestershire. Impulsive as ever, she bought a horrific bungalow near Pershore, with traffic roaring past, polystyrene ceilings, plywood doors and sludge-coloured kitchen and bathroom tiles, embossed with pink roses; she realized at once that she had made the most fearful mistake, and begged me to join her on interminable visits to the bungalow, during the course of which I urged her to get rid of it immediately, and not waste another penny on remedying the irremediable. Not surprisingly, perhaps, she had become more volatile and irascible than ever. She complained of headaches and problems with her specs, and seemed to be suffering from paranoia, sniffing conspiracies in the most improbable places; down in the cottage one evening, she became convinced that

Mrs X – a long-suffering friend who endlessly put herself out on Barbara's behalf, and had built an elaborate cage in the back garden to prevent the pussers from being mown down by passing traffic – had, on purpose, stolen the cork out of a wine bottle, and nothing I could say would persuade her otherwise. Her doctors, happy to dismiss her as a difficult and neurotic woman, pumped up her doses of anti-depressants; but Petra, sensing something far more serious, urged her to get a second opinion. On our last trip back from the bungalow, the pussers howling in the back, Barbara was so querulous and bad-tempered that, more than once, I offered to get out and take the train home. 'Well, *that's* the end of a beautiful friendship,' she told Petra as she stormed into our house, where a belated lunch was waiting. We never met again, and I've always regretted, terribly, that we parted on such bad terms; a few days later she was told that she had a tumour on the brain, and after a spell in the Cromwell Hospital, where I tried but failed to see her, Clive Donner and Jocelyn Rickards took her down to Cressida Connolly's house in the country, where she died surrounded by the people she loved most in the world. Some time later, I was presented with a complete transcript of those troublesome letters by a mutual friend who knew how much I wanted to read them, could decipher Connolly's spidery scrawl, was a far quicker typist than I could ever be, and – miraculously – had managed to put them in some kind of order after much quizzing of postmarks and the like; they were not the most edifying documents, with Connolly revealing himself at his most treacherous and self-pitying, but without them my biography would have been very much the poorer.

That was not the end of the affair. Barbara had also given me various diaries and papers of her own, and these included some unkind remarks about her second husband, George Weidenfeld.

Although she had left Connolly for his publisher, with whom she had become briefly infatuated, their marriage had been a brief and wretched affair. I knew, from Alan Ross, how upset Weidenfeld had been by her account of their relationship in her memoirs; and now I was not only reopening old wounds, but adding second-hand salt of my own. After I had finished my book, I sent Lord Weidenfeld the relevant pages with a note saying how sorry I was to bring all this up once more, and asking if he could bear to check it for inaccuracies. The weeks went by, and I heard nothing. Cape wanted to get the book into production; I dreaded a writ for libel, or a terrible cry of rage. I got home one evening, and my youngest daughter, Hattie, told me that a foreign-sounding man had rung a couple of times: could I ring him back? Heart pounding, I picked up the phone and rang Weidenfeld at his home on Chelsea Embankment. A purring, slightly inflected voice told me that the chapter I had sent him was most elegantly done, that he was full of admiration; when I apologized for raising old ghosts he assured me that I should not worry, that it was all ancient history, but would I mind terribly if he suggested some very small corrections? 'Of course not,' I cried, bending low with gratitude and pleasure. He hoped I wouldn't mind, but a particular date was wrong: no problem. I had misquoted from the Latin: I had always been hopeless at Latin, and was more than happy to stand corrected. Was there anything else in need of amendment? Well, he said, it was rather a pity that I'd made mention of – and here he referred to some unkind but comical observation of Barbara's, culled from the papers she had left me rather than the published memoirs. It wasn't libellous, and I was loath to lose it, so I said nothing, and the conversation moved elsewhere. 'Now,' he suddenly said, 'I'm going to tell you something in the strictest confidence, and you're not to use it in your book. Do you know who told me, when I was in New York, that

Barbara had left me and returned to Cyril?' I didn't, and begged
him to reveal all about this key moment in Connolly's career. It
was, he said, Caroline Blackwood: but that was for my ears only.
This was, from my point of view, a fact well worth the knowing:
while married to Barbara, Connolly was always hoping to seduce
Caroline Blackwood, earning himself a sharp kick in the buttocks
from Lucian Freud in the process. Since Caroline Blackwood had
recently died, it seemed innocuous enough: but although, unlike
the waspish aside to which Lord Weidenfeld had objected, it was
a small but valuable part of the jigsaw, I'd promised not to use it;
and that, it seemed, was that.

After I put the phone down, I wrote George Weidenfeld a brief
note to thank him for his generosity about both my writing and
the resurrection of some painful memories; I also begged him to
reconsider about Caroline Blackwood, while assuring him that
my lips were sealed unless he changed his mind. A day or two
later the phone rang, and the great publisher was on the line. He
had a proposal to make, and I craned eagerly forward in my
chair: if I would remove that waspish observation of Barbara's, he
would allow me to include the Blackwood revelation. I was more
than happy to accept his terms; yet although I was immensely
relieved to be able to go ahead, my overriding feeling was one of
liking and admiration for my partner in the deal, whatever
Barbara's views on the matter. I had always thought him the most
glamorous and intelligent of publishers, a worldly, empurpled
Renaissance pontiff adrift at a Methodist meeting, and now he
had joined my pantheon of heroes.

Like many other writers – Auden most famously so – my old
friend and colleague D. J. Enright abominated literary biographies: what mattered about writers was their work, not their
lives, and lives of writers, unless written by the subjects themselves, were intrusive, trivial, irrelevant and somehow immoral.

He enjoyed reading my memoirs (or 'me-moirs' as he called them), but although he always asked politely enough how I was getting on with my biography of Cyril Connolly, he did so between gritted teeth, and I would hurriedly change the subject in favour of cats (a shared enthusiasm), or the bad old days when we had suffered together at Chatto & Windus. Since Dennis died at the end of 2002, I have published a biography of Smollett, and now I'm hard at work on a life of Allen Lane. I have loved every minute of both; and although half of me still shares Dennis's disapproval, the other half has been utterly corrupted. I only hope his shade doesn't disapprove too much.

Margaret Forster

Rebecca's Ghost

Why did I choose Daphne du Maurier as a subject for a biography? I don't believe that I did. I never met her, never corresponded with her and she had almost certainly never even heard of me; and yet, in the strangest way, a series of remarkable coincidences convinced me that she chose me.

What happened was this. One Sunday morning, 16 April 1989, I was reaching up for a book on the top shelf of a bookcase when another volume fell down. I picked it up and saw that it was *Rebecca*, which I hadn't read since I was about 13. I stood there, reading again that famous opening sequence, remembering how it had thrilled me, and found myself wondering if Daphne du Maurier was still alive and whether there was a biography of her. Biography was very much on my mind. I longed to embark on another, but ever since I had finished working on Elizabeth Barrett Browning, a subject for another had eluded me. Novels, for me at least, begin in a natural way – they 'boil up in the interior' as W. M. Thackeray once put it – but biographies are different, and have much more artificial starting points. By 1989, I had written three biographies and knew that what I liked best was literary biography – all that lovely reading of the work – but that I wanted to get out of the nineteenth century and into the twentieth, into my own times. What I wanted most of all was to be the first – first at the letters and diaries nobody had seen, first to analyse the work, first to mark the way. I wanted to be the authorized biographer of a writer who had just died, or who was likely to. But no recently dead writer had inspired me, and I was marking time, waiting.

So there I stood, that April day, suddenly feeling excited –
Daphne du Maurier, of course, the perfect subject! How many
novels had she written? I didn't know, but I knew that *Rebecca*
wasn't the only good one. There was *My Cousin Rachel*, and
Jamaica Inn, and *Frenchman's Creek*, and *The House on the Strand*,
and I had a recollection that as well as novels she had written a
couple of biographies too, one of them about Branwell Brontë. I
knew she lived in Cornwall, and was reclusive (if still alive), and
that her father had been a famous actor-manager. I looked her up
in *The Oxford Companion to English Literature* (1985): five pretty
dismissive lines, mentioning only *Rebecca*, and yet I was sure she
had had an enormous influence on that much-despised genre,
'popular' fiction. But *Rebecca*, if my memory served me correctly,
was more than 'popular'. Snobbery at work, then?

I sat down and wrote a postcard to Carmen Callil, my then
publisher, asking her if she knew whether Daphne du Maurier
was still alive, and whether she thought she'd be a good subject
for a biography by me. I went out and posted it immediately, then
spent the afternoon re-reading *Rebecca*. Next day, I was on to *My
Cousin Rachel*, and I had been to the library and made a list of all
Daphne du Maurier's books. The following morning, Tuesday
18 April, there was a card back from Carmen – 'Terrific idea!' –
saying that Daphne du Maurier was still alive, and that she knew
her agent and would suggest me as a biographer straight away. I
read *Jamaica Inn* that evening. On Wednesday, around midday, I
had a telephone call from a producer on *Kaleidoscope*, the Radio 4
Arts programme of the day: would I come in and do an on-the-
spot obituary/appreciation of Daphne du Maurier, who had just
died. Hardly had I put the phone down, after agreeing, than there
was another call, from *The Sunday Times*, asking if I would do
their obituary of her. Coincidences, all of them, three in a row,
but they struck me as odd. There were plenty of *Kaleidoscope*

contributors for producers to think of, and as for *The Sunday Times*, I had never done an obituary for them (or anyone else) in my life. Yet the strangest coincidence of all was the first, that at the precise moment *Rebecca* fell off my shelf, Daphne du Maurier was beginning to organize her own death. For the six previous weeks, she had eaten virtually nothing. She had accepted drinks of Complan but would touch nothing else, and was down to six stone. On Sunday 16 April, when she got up she said she wanted to be taken down to the beach where Rebecca had met her death. The weather, even though it was April, was savage that day, with a wild wind blowing and rain driving in from the sea. But her nurse, Margaret, drove her to the track leading to the beach and helped her out, both of them staggering against the wind. Daphne stood there for a while, with Margaret in the background, staring out to sea: a tragic figure, frail and silent. Then she got Margaret to take her to visit Veronica Rashleigh and a series of other friends, to whom she bade farewell. Everyone who saw her on that day and during the next one was convinced she was trying to control what happened in her life.

I didn't, of course, know all this when I applied to become Daphne du Maurier's authorized biographer but I loved the feeling of fate somehow having intervened. I kept Carmen's postcard, with its date stamp wonderfully clear, or I might have come to believe I had made this beginning up. It wasn't, though, the actual beginning because it took the family nine months to agree that I should be allowed to write the biography. People perhaps don't realize how competitive contemporary biography can be – someone of note dies, and the vultures circle. Proposals have to be written and presented and scrutinized, terms agreed, and in this case a good deal of agonizing gone through on the part of the literary executors about whether Daphne du Maurier's wish that there should not be a biography could be overridden. Fortunately for me, it was declared that her anti-biography stance only applied to when she was alive. I am sure this was right. I found later plenty of proof that she valued biography so long as it was truthful. What she could not bear were biographies that were what she called 'stereotyped, dull as ditch-water, or very fulsome praising'. Her own biography of her father was an example of that 'all truth' she wanted – bold, opinionated, admiring but highly critical.

It was a good thing that it took so long for me to be appointed Daphne du Maurier's biographer, though with two unauthorized biographies appearing within that time, it did not seem so. The waiting, after the romantic start, made me quite sure that I wanted to embark on the project. There has to be a strong sense of commitment, it seems to me, because there is so much work involved – novels (mine) take weeks, or at the most a few months, but biographies take years. Slipping into the life of another is not easy, but once into it nothing else exists, it is obsessive and demanding and worrying. All very well to talk about coincidences, and make it all sound so casual and light-hearted, but the undertaking is overwhelming. I wanted to go where no one had gone before, but when it came to that 'marking of the way' I had so longed to do, I was often bewildered and longed for the direction others could have given me if they had been the first.

There was one last 'coincidence' (I can't help putting it like that because I still want to believe it wasn't coincidence at all – silly, but true). Four years later, when my biography was finally published, I had to prepare myself for appearing at those events which promote the book. This isn't something I usually do, hating all the publicity (just as Daphne did) but I knew that some of the discoveries I had made and written about were going to attract a lot of attention, and that this was likely to be hostile. I felt that I had to stand by my own book, and justify its conclusions. So for once I agreed to speak at literary lunches and dinners in nine different cities, and to do that I had to look my best. This meant buying new clothes, which in turn meant shopping for them. Again, like Daphne, I loathe shopping, but off I set, determined to find some outfits sufficiently presentable. Ordinary chain stores are my limit – I wasn't thinking designer labels – so I trawled Oxford Street and then Bond Street. In Fenwick's, I found a dress, but it needed a jacket. Finally, I settled on a very stylish red linen jacket, but there was no price tag on it. I took it to the cash desk, and said I wanted it but needed to know the price. The assistant said the tag was in the inside pocket, which I hadn't even noticed was there, and she pulled it out and showed it to me. The price was on one side and on the other was the name Rebecca with underneath the name of the designer. Every time I had to speak at some event during the next few weeks, I would put my hand in the pocket and close it around this tag, and imagine Daphne laughing.

Andrew Motion

Breaking In

In September 1946, when he was 24, Philip Larkin went to work as sub-librarian at University College, Leicester. Within three weeks he had met Monica Jones, a lecturer in the English Department. After three years they had become lovers. After another six months Larkin left Leicester for the library at Queen's University, Belfast, where he stayed for five years, seeing Monica regularly but at widely spaced intervals. In 1955 he was appointed Librarian at the University of Hull, and remained there for the last 30 years of his life. During this time he and Monica took annual holidays together, met at least once a month, wrote to each other and/or spoke on the telephone nearly every day. The relationship was in certain respects deeply troubled (by jealousies, by distance), and in others very happy. Monica was Larkin's steadfast companion and his soul-mate. He dedicated *The Less Deceived* to her: it was the only collection of poems he dedicated to anyone.

In September 1961 Monica bought a small house in Haydon Bridge near Northumberland, on the main Newcastle–Carlisle road. (Her family had originally come from that part of the world.) She meant it to be a bolt-hole – somewhere she might escape the various worries of her private life and her university work. Larkin was initially suspicious of the house but soon admiring. He took holidays there, hunkered down in it for weekends, always visited at New Year. When he wouldn't or couldn't leave Hull, Monica was often in Haydon Bridge alone – writing Larkin letters, waiting for him to ring. The house was their special place, their burrow.

In June 1983, when she was 61, recently retired from Leicester, and living in Haydon Bridge more or less full time, Monica developed shingles. Larkin, who was staying, took charge. He ferried her south to Hull and put her in hospital, where she lay half-blinded and in great pain for several days. Then he brought her back to his own house in Hull. She stayed ten months – until the following April – before returning to Haydon Bridge, meaning to restart her independent life. But she was still unwell, and anyway Larkin missed her. Within a few days he had decided to collect her again. He helped her pack, then sat in the car while she checked for last things, drew the curtains, switched off the electricity at the meter, and locked the front door. Anxiously, he drove her back to Hull.

Larkin thought Monica was fatally ill. In fact, he was. Within a year he was in hospital for tests; on 2 December 1985 he died of cancer. Monica stayed in Hull – depressed, sick and exhausted. She wanted her own life back but was too ill to get herself there.

Early in 1986 Monica asked me to write a biography of Larkin, and over the next few years we saw a great deal of each other. She sat in what had once been Larkin's chair, his tweed coat still slung over the arm. I sat on the sofa, his Rowlandson watercolour on the dark green wall behind me. Sometimes I formally inter-viewed her; sometimes we just chatted. Sometimes we looked at photographs of him or by him; sometimes we read his books. There was no hurry. She had known Larkin better than anyone. I had to ransack her memory.

Monica said nothing about the letters Larkin had written her. If I asked where they were, she would shrug – lighting another cigarette, pouring another drink. Did this mean she didn't want me to see them? Or had they, like his diaries, been destroyed? She wasn't telling.

One day out of the blue she said most of the letters were in Haydon Bridge. Why didn't we drive up together to get them? It was a forlorn hope – she was too ill – yet she didn't want me to go without her. The house was theirs: a secret place, where she and Larkin had lived to the exclusion of all others. Dark-curtained and unvisited, it held their continuing, unbroken life together. Once the door had been opened, that life would be over.

Months passed. Monica grew more frail. Eventually she decided I would have to go alone. I drove up with a friend from Hull, Marion Shaw, in the autumn of 1989. As far as I knew, no one had been into the house for five years.

We roller-coastered the wet road towards Hexham, then on. Rain was swirling in from the North Sea behind us. So much had fallen in recent weeks, the moors were yellow and sour-looking. As we ducked down into Haydon Bridge, streams bulged in the ditches beside us.

The house was even smaller than I'd expected, and uglier. Packed into a tight row near the Old Bridge, on the main road, it had a jaded white front, a slate roof, plain modern windows and a front door which opened straight off the street. I got the key from a neighbour and opened up – but the door was stuck. Peering through the letter-box, the rain falling on my neck and back, I could see why. There was a mound of junk mail on the mat: offers of free film, estate agents' bumf, cards from taxi companies and window cleaners.

I shoved the door violently and we were in. A tiny box of a hall, the sitting-room to the left, stairs rising straight ahead. The stairs looked crazy. There was no carpet (just the pale section where a carpet had once been), and at the sides of each step, cans of food. One of these had leaked, oozing blood-coloured treacle into a puddle at my feet. I tried to wipe it up, scrape it up, somehow get rid of it, with a piece of junk mail. It was impossible. In the end I hid it beneath a few bright envelopes.

The smell was worse when I turned on the electricity. Sweet open-air dampness like a rotten log – but also fusty. And there was noise too, noise I couldn't recognize. A roaring, but somehow subdued. When I turned into the sitting-room I understood. Outside the window at the back, beyond a cramped cement yard and a towpath, there flowed a gigantic river: the Tyne, invisible from the road. Within the first few seconds of looking, I saw a full-grown tree sweep past, then heard the trunk grinding against the bridge away to my left, out of sight.

The window was broken – a hole like a star-burst and slivers of glass on the purple carpet.

We weren't the first people here for years, we were the second and third. The drawers in a sideboard lolled open, empty; in the grate, jagged pieces of crockery poked out of a sootfall; there was a dark circle in the dust on a table where a vase had stood. And there were books all over the floor – books flung about for the hell of it – and a deep scar on the window seat where something heavy had been manhandled into the yard then away along the towpath.

We tiptoed through the shambles, closing up, straightening, tidying, our hands immediately grey with dust. It was wet dust, sticking to us and clinging in our noses and lungs. Monica hadn't told me where I might find the letters, but it didn't matter. They were everywhere. In books, down the side of a chair, under a rug, on the window seat. A few lay flat and saturated in the yard, scrabbled out when the last burglar left.

It was the same upstairs, though the dust seemed lighter there, maybe because the rain had eased off outside and the sun was starting to break through. The river sounded quieter, too, and I could see a family on the opposite bank – a man, a woman and two children, walking a dog.

I went into the lumber room, into a jungle of clothes and hangers which had a small box at its heart, stuffed with letters.

Nothing in the bathroom.

In the smaller bedroom: under the window overlooking the river, a bed with letters both inside and underneath it, and a cupboard crowded with damp dresses which tore when I touched them.

In the larger bedroom: more letters in books, an empty case of wine, an ironing board with a half-ironed dress draped across it.

When I got downstairs I realized I was breathing in gulps, as if I were swimming.

We counted the letters into plastic bags. There were nearly 200 of them. Then we went through the house again, found the last handful, turned off the electricity, locked up, returned the key to the neighbour, arranged for the window to be repaired and climbed into the car. The sun had gone in; it was starting to rain again. Larkin had sat in the same place, squinnying at the little house, feeling anxious. I felt exhilarated and ashamed.

I wasn't the last. A week or so after I'd taken the letters back to Monica, a van drew up outside the house in Haydon Bridge and two people got out, kicked open the front door and stole nearly everything inside. If the letters had still been there, they would have gone too. By the time this happened, I'd read them – and 200 or so more, that Monica revealed Larkin had written to her in Leicester.

Diarmaid MacCulloch

Archives

Like most of my writing projects, my biography of Thomas
Cranmer was someone else's idea: Virginia Murphy, a friend and
former fellow-student of Sir Geoffrey Elton who had gone on to
be a publisher, suggested the project. I found her proposal particularly attractive because it seemed the perfect way to learn about
the early Reformation in England: Cranmer was at the centre of
everything that had happened, and so in meeting him, I would
meet everyone else who mattered at the time. Nevertheless, when
I started reading on Cranmer, I was intimidated by the competition. In 1905 A. F. Pollard produced an outstanding biography in
his series of studies of the great names of Tudor England. It is
noticeably fair-minded, particularly in a masterly chapter on
'Cranmer's character and private Life'. Cranmer was again well
served by Jasper Ridley in 1962, in what is probably the best of all
Ridley's numerous biographies. So was there anything more to
say?

As I began gathering material and then writing the final text, I
was reassured. I did have a number of lucky new archival finds,
but more interesting was the way in which the whole body of
material on Cranmer (most of it long in the public arena) began
pulling me towards a picture which I had not found in the
existing biographies. The evidence had been there, but it had not
been treated with the perspective I now found being thrust upon
me, a perspective still taking shape as I brought my text to a close.
In the past, Cranmer had usually been treated as an English
churchman with a few foreign friends, rather than as a major
player in a European-wide revolution, with a cosmopolitan

outlook exceptional among his English contemporaries. In Cranmer, I found a man who brought up a Polish boy in his archiepiscopal household during the 1530s, who took a German Lutheran as his second wife, who even before he had been chosen as Archbishop, had established a number of friendships with evangelical leaders overseas, whose favourite printer in London was from Strassburg, and who while he was Archbishop of Canterbury, maintained something like his own intelligence service right across Europe, as far away as Rome.

All this alerted me to how un-Anglican Cranmer was. The Reformation he created was part of a larger event, and its nearest relative was the Strassburg of the contemporary reformer Martin Bucer, whom Cranmer first contacted as early as 1531, before he attained the see of Canterbury. Cranmer had no affection for many of the things which give Anglicanism its particular character today. He showed no enthusiasm for cathedrals and their music, and would have been unsympathetic to the performance of choral evensong which is one of the chief glories of the modern Anglican tradition – that was not to say that he was not cultured, because his new buildings and even the design of the seals on his documents reveal an exceptionally advanced Renaissance taste. In theology, he had no time for ideas of apostolic succession of the episcopate, a notion which has come to hold great importance in Anglicanism. His theology was structured by predestination, a theological concept which Anglicanism has on the whole decided to treat with caution. He would have been shocked by the idea of a 'via media' between Rome and Protestantism; one cannot have a via media between Antichrist and truth.

The Anglo-Catholics who had dominated Anglican historical writing for more than a century were therefore justified in deploring Cranmer, within their own framework of reference. It had been in no one's interest to point out obvious facts about him since the seventeenth century, and every reason as Anglicanism constructed its tribal identity to enrol the chief actor in the English Reformation as a rather more than honorary Anglican. It was with the foreignness of Cranmer in mind that I chose the picture for the dust-jacket of my book: a picture of the man himself. I took not the well-known 1545 portrait of him by Gerlach Flicke in the National Portrait Gallery, but a later bearded portrait of the Archbishop in Lambeth Palace. That had been the normative image of him until the late seventeenth century, but Anglicans had found that it gave Cranmer an alarming resemblance to European Protestant Reformers such as Heinrich Bullinger or John Calvin. So bearded Cranmer from Edward VI's turbulent Protestant church was replaced with the smooth-faced image from the reign of Henry VIII.

But at the end of all the writing, after I had written some quarter of a million words, chosen the dust-jacket for the book and apparently ended my labours, there came a revelation which might have proved disastrous. In fact it turned out sensationally and satisfyingly to confirm what had gone before. The first proofs of the book arrived from Yale University Press, in the middle of a busy university term. As I began reading them, I got a letter from Dr Stephen Ryle, a lecturer in Classics at Leeds University. I did not know Ryle at all, but he had happened to meet another academic friend of mine, who mentioned to him that I was writing a life of Cranmer. Ryle, with enormous generosity and altruism, was now writing to ask me if I knew of a couple of letters of Thomas Cranmer which he had found in a library in Cracow. He enclosed photocopies of the originals. All this I took in at a glance and with a sinking heart at the beginning of a crowded Friday, full of wall-to-wall lecturing and tutoring. It was only at the end of that exhausting day, haunted throughout by the glimpse of those photocopies and the knowledge that I might have to rethink a great deal of what I had written, that I could take the full measure of what was there.

The photocopies were daunting: two letters scrawled in a sixteenth-century Polish secretary-hand, very different from the western European handwriting with which I was familiar, and written in the laid-back classical Latin of one sophisticated humanist writing to another. I spent a feverish weekend reading the photocopies, transcribing and translating the Latin, and considering what their significance might be for me and for Cranmer. The effort was worth it. The letters were a revelation: far away in Poland, in a fragment of the archives of the Polish royal house which had survived all the destruction and disasters of Polish history even through the Second World War, there remained these documents which threw a shaft of light across Tudor history – totally unknown to Tudor historians because of their exotic location. They were the earliest letters of Thomas Cranmer's which I had seen: he wrote them in 1527 to a new friend he had made while on a royal mission to the Holy Roman Emperor in Spain, the Polish ambassador Johannes Dantiscus. Dantiscus had ordered a secretary to transcribe the letters for the benefit of the King of Poland, evidently because they included scraps of diplomatic gossip about Henry VIII's daughter, the Princess Mary.

The gossip was not primarily what mattered to me. The letters revealed Thomas Cranmer as one of the main delegates of a high-profile diplomatic mission from Tudor England, at a time when the history books had left him as a quiet Cambridge don, as yet unknown on the national stage. No other modern historian had suspected that he had been in Spain, for there appears to be no other mention of his presence there (perhaps some Spanish archive might still reveal more). Here was a cosmopolitan diplomat who had enough social graces to strike up a friendship with Dantiscus, notoriously one of the most festive men in Europe as well as an internationally known Latin poet. We had a few glimpses in some later letters of their friendship (which eventually ended coldly in 1540 when Dantiscus had become a defender of the old faith as a bishop back in Poland), but there had been no hint as to how long and why the two men had known each other. Cranmer's letters of 1527 went on to describe his first meeting with King Henry VIII, two years earlier than we had other evidence of any contact between them, after the English diplomat had endured an epic stormy voyage across the Bay of Biscay. When Cranmer came into Henry's presence and made his report, the King gave him a ring as a token of royal favour, just as he would do in 1543 to save Cranmer's life amid the 'Prebendaries' Plot', one of the greatest crises of the Archbishop's career.

Not only did the letters fit into a blank period of Cranmer's life, to my huge relief they fitted a newly revised picture of those early years which I had glimpsed through other fragments of evidence, and which I had already placed at the beginning of Cranmer's story. Traditional historical clichés had tried to hurry the Cambridge don on to being a Protestant as soon as possible, more or less as soon as news of Martin Luther had reached Cambridge in the early 1520s. Other dons who became great names of the English Reformation like Hugh Latimer had certainly made this rapid leap from old world to new, and in the past, Cranmer had been rather unthinkingly added to the list. But it had become clear to me that Cranmer had moved more slowly; his circle of friends and even some of the marginal comments in one of his surviving books suggested a rather traditionalist academic in those first years of Reformation tumult. Now through the Cracow letters, my Cranmer was revealed as a recruit to Cardinal Wolsey's diplomatic corps, like other Cambridge dons of his generation. Wolsey would never have employed a man for a mission to the Holy Roman Emperor who was not a reliable Catholic. So in 1527 Cranmer was not at all as yet a Protestant reformer, but he was already a man with an international vision, linked through Dantiscus to the most fashionable men of humanist culture in the Continent. The Polish boy at Lambeth Palace through the 1530s did not seem so puzzling after all.

I held the proofs back for a few days, and when I had sorted out the story in my mind, I wrote various new sections of text which would take account of the 'Ryle' letters from Cracow. What was particularly satisfying is that these new insertions fitted snugly into the existing text. They enriched a story which had already been presented to me by the evidence already in place: I had already found a conservative but cosmopolitan humanist who underwent a quite sudden conversion to the Protestant revolution around 1531, during the crisis of Henry VIII's repudiation of Queen Katherine of Aragon. Yet all through his Protestant years, Cranmer never lost his sense of being part of a continent-wide culture of scholarship and theological debate. So rewriting the proofs was much less painful than might have proved the case. Robert Baldock, most sympathetic and supportive of editors, quite rightly charged me 60 pounds for the disruption and delay to Yale's production schedule, but we knew that it was money well spent. My Cranmer had become a richer, more rounded figure – and he had become more like the Cranmer whom I had already been sketching. Cranmer is still a very quiet, hidden man, but now at least one of his seven veils has slipped to the ground. I still hope that the archives will take the dance further.

Hilary Spurling

Glendower's Syndrome

The great Romantic biographer, Richard Holmes, sees himself as a ferryman plying back and forth over the waters of oblivion between the living and the dead. More contemporary practitioners, like me, get called by nastier names – scavenger, jackal, vampire, garbage-collector – all of them valid up to a point. But sometimes I feel more like Shakespeare's Welshman, Owen Glendower, who exasperated Hotspur in *Henry IV Part I* by claiming he could call spirits from the vasty deep. 'Why, so can I, or so can any man,' Hotspur snapped back smartly, 'but *will they come* when you do call for them?'

All twentieth-century biographers spend long hours calling up the dead not just with the help of letters, diaries, books and documentary records but through the use of living human mediums. Like any form of séance, this can be a dodgy business, open to distortion if not fakery, often disconcerting and always unpredictable on the rare occasions when it works, as it has done for me twice, or possibly three times in my life. The first time I was totally unprepared. I was learning the trade by writing a first biography of Ivy Compton-Burnett, who had just died in 1969 at the age of 85. Dame Ivy insisted that her life was too dull to write about. She refused to talk to anyone about her early years, corresponded with her friends on laconic postcards, and took the precaution of destroying all her papers. Her novels, invariably set in the period of her own youth before the First World War, explore the consequences of sexual and financial malfunction, submerged violence and the abuse of power within large inward-turned families almost entirely devoid of contact with the outside world. A little preliminary research at the central record office in London showed that Ivy was the seventh child in a family of thirteen by two different mothers. Neither she nor any of her brothers and sisters produced children. Three of the thirteen killed themselves. The only survivors, after Ivy died, were two unmarried younger sisters living together in a cottage in the Hertfordshire countryside.

Miss Vera and Miss Judy Compton-Burnett, both then approaching 80, turned out to be still going strong as joint head-mistresses of a Rudolph Steiner school at King's Langley (their ex-pupils, I discovered later, included Jonathan Miller and the cartoonist Nicholas Garland). They sent their regular taxi-driver to collect me from the station, and I asked him nervously what they were like. 'Oh yes,' he said, instantly grasping the question I was not sure how to put directly: 'Oh yes, those two are the Big I Ams round here.' They were brisk, upright, commanding ladies with teacosy white hairdos like their sister, and the welcome they gave me at their rather austere tea-table could not have been kinder. Miss Vera, the elder and more vocal of the two, announced firmly that they had nothing to tell me. She and her sister had seen little of Ivy for over 50 years, had never spent a night under the same roof since they grew up, and had wasted no time as adults thinking about the childhood and adolescence they had shared together before the Compton-Burnett household finally fell apart in 1915. Over tea we talked about Steiner's educational theory, the different coloured auras possessed by all human beings, and the importance of not teaching a child anything it might not want to learn. I had brought two little flowering pot-plants, one of which the sisters greeted with glad cries, giving it a drink and a saucer to sit on at the table. 'Oh Vera, look!' cried Miss Judy, spotting the other, still sitting forlornly in its paper wrapper on the sideboard as we got up from the table:

'this one's been forgotten. *Just like the stepchild.*' My heartbeat gave a little jump.

We adjourned across the garden to the study. This was a substantial shed-like building furnished with massive wooden chests and cupboards carved in the Steiner style without straight lines, like domestic furnishings left over from *Lord of the Rings*. 'Ask us whatever you like,' said Miss Vera as soon as we were settled: 'Judy and I talked about the old days last night, and we can't remember anything.' I started with simple queries about life in the Compton-Burnett nursery – meals, walks, rules, the games they played, the clothes they wore, and the nurse who looked after them – moving on to the various groups and sub-groups in their strictly hierarchical Victorian family: Ivy herself and two brothers with a governess in the schoolroom, the older stepsisters downstairs in the drawing-room, the big stepbrothers longing to leave home, the servants segregated in the basement. Then there were the parents, both formidable figures, whose long shadows can still be sensed in the background to Ivy's novels.

This initial meeting, which none of us had expected to repeat, became the first of many question-and-answer sessions conducted in that garden study by the dim green light of early evening before the taxi came back to fetch me at seven. For all three of us it was like opening a door that had been closed for more than half a century, and stepping through it into unknown territory that looked increasingly familiar as more and more of it came into view. We approached from opposite directions. I had always loved Ivy's novels, and knew them almost by heart at that point. Her sisters had never read any of the books but, as they slowly pieced together their forgotten childhood, I recognized the landscape, and the figures in it, clearly enough in the mirror of Ivy's fiction. They were as fascinated as I was by the process. For a year and a half I visited them regularly, arriving once a month in time for tea, after which we crossed the garden to enter a world of memory and imagination, a place where the shapes and forces of Ivy's fictional reality confronted the factual sources emerging from her sisters' memories, which grew with time steadily clearer, brighter and more sharply focused.

The Compton-Burnett family, shaken and eventually destroyed by a series of traumatic shocks in the years leading up to 1914, had finally split up a year later when Vera and Judy ran away with their two youngest sisters to set up home together in London. For Ivy, the secrets of the early life she never mentioned fed into the rich compost of her novels. For Vera and Judy, absorbed by the practical demands of parallel teaching careers, the same secrets had been overlaid, lying concealed beneath the conscious level of their minds, unvisited but intact, to be eventually retrieved in the company of a stranger after half a century, when their power to wound or threaten had been cauterized by time. I was often amazed at how readily my hostesses answered questions so painful and disturbing I found them difficult to ask. It was 18 months before I could bring myself to probe the double suicide of the two youngest girls, Primrose and Topsy Compton-Burnett, aged 18 and 21 when they swallowed overdoses of veronal in bed together on Christmas Day, 1917, behind a locked door in the flat they shared with Vera and Judy. No one who knew them ever talked about why or how they died, at the time or afterwards, and there were no surviving police or coroner's records of what *The Times* reported as MYSTERY IN ST JOHN'S WOOD.

I finally raised the matter with their sisters at what proved to be our final working session together. 'I'm so glad you brought that up,' said Vera, explaining that they had never discussed the deaths before, even with one another. Judy said she vividly remembered the leaves turning colour on the trees, which meant

the girls must have died in early autumn. This showed the protective and evasive power of memory, even at that late stage, for
in fact the Home Office post-mortem set the date of death as two
days before the discovery of the bodies on 27 December. Both
sisters were eager to learn more, so we ended our last session
with me answering their questions (from death certificates
and contemporary newspaper reports) about what actually
happened. We met again as friends, but the purely social visits I
paid later had none of the intensity or urgency of those earlier
séances when between us we uncovered a half-suspected story –
buried deep by them, partially dug up by me – that engrossed us
all.

My second subject was Paul Scott, who wrote the four extraordinary novels known as the *Raj Quartet*, televised in the 1980s
as *The Jewel in the Crown*. Unlike Ivy, Paul both talked and wrote
freely about his work and life. I had no difficulty finding close
friends only too glad to tell me all they knew, and the Scott family
gave me unrestricted access to his private papers – 12,000 documents in all – stored at the University of Tulsa, Oklahoma, where
I spent six weeks reading them with growing astonishment. I had
arrived in Tulsa with only the vaguest outline map of the life in
question in my head. But the more I knew, the less I understood.
Paul's letters were shrewd, intimate and highly revealing, but the
secrets they discussed were always other people's. So far as his
own inner life was concerned, he might as well have destroyed
everything, like Ivy. The Tulsa correspondence came to seem to
me more like an elaborate smokescreen, concealing rather than
revealing crucial information without which I could make no
sense of his life on any but the most superficial level.

It was as if I had assembled a large and complicated jigsaw
puzzle only to find a key piece missing. I didn't know what I was
looking for, or where it might be found, unless it was in the only

area of his life I had not already searched. This was the 20 months after he was conscripted into the army in 1940, and before he sailed as a young officer cadet for India on a voyage that would change his life for ever. He never mentioned this period himself, and it proved almost impossible to trace. There were no army records of civilian conscripts, and the only people with whom Paul had kept in contact at this time were the poet Clive Sansom, who was dead, and his wife, an Australian now living in Hobart, Tasmania. Ruth Sansom and I exchanged letters. She was friendly, helpful, delighted to answer any questions I cared to put about the past, but unable to cast light on anything that might solve my problem. She urged me to visit her all the same, and in desperation I arranged to fly halfway round the world on a hunch I could not justify, even to myself.

I tacked ten days in Tasmania on to the end of a research trip already planned to retrace Paul's footsteps across India. At times on that trip I felt like a ghost myself, especially when I stayed alone at the hotel just outside the hill station of Belgaum in the Western ghats, where he had set his Booker Prize-winning novel, *Staying On*. The last European to stay there before me was probably Paul himself nearly 20 years earlier. There was no fax or telephone, and no one to answer letters, so I had no way of booking a room beforehand, which hardly mattered in the end because the building, unchanged since Paul left, lay empty and deserted. The life of the hotel had shifted to the compound, where half the male population of the nearby town gathered at night on weekends to drink and talk. When I arrived one Saturday afternoon, dressed in the kind of Raj-style white linen outfit fashionable throughout Britain in the late 1980s, I must have looked like a revenant from a past neither I nor any of these young men had ever known. They put me in a huge, high, bare, dusty room – the famous Room Number One in *Staying On* –

containing nothing now except a vast double bedstead enveloped in an ancient mosquito net suspended from the ceiling, elephant-grey, the size and shape of a bell-tent. The bedroom door, divided in two like a stable-door, would not shut. I was the only woman on the premises. All night I lay and listened to the tramp of bare feet as the hotel's staff and customers came to my door, one by one, eager to see for themselves this ghostly reminder of a British memsahib, who had washed up out of nowhere in their midst.

Three weeks later I reached Hobart, where Ruth Sansom had insisted that I stay in her tiny bungalow on the slopes of Mount Wellington just above the town. She was a Quaker, already in her 70s, teetotal and stone deaf. I had brought her a bottle of Maharashtra champagne and a peacock feather fan which I quickly swapped for a warm Kashmiri shawl and some packets of tea. She started to talk at once about her husband, Clive, as an aspiring poet before the Second World War, and his 19-year-old protegé, the would-be poet, Paul Scott. I listened, prompting, responding and scribbling further questions on bits of paper. Our conversation lasted throughout my stay. We saw practically no one, and seldom left the house, which had a tree of ripe nectarines in the garden and a spectacular view over Hobart Bay. Inside it we reconstructed what went on long ago between those three young people in another house on a North London hillside, the house in Southgate where Ruth spent the last months of peace with Clive and Paul before all their lives were finally disrupted by the war.

For ten days we talked and thought of nothing else. I had much to tell her. In return, her memory stirred and expanded, releasing things she had not spoken of or thought about for years, some of them things she had not realized she knew, and certainly had had no means of understanding at the time. Clive and Paul, viewed from this distant vantage point in time and space, became in some ways more distinct than they could ever have been to the young Ruth. The missing piece in the puzzle of Paul's life fell into place. By the time I left, we were both exhausted, but we had seen them clear and whole, and felt their presence as strongly as if they had just stepped outside, or were perhaps still there in the next room. On my last night but one, Ruth laid four places without thinking at the supper table instead of two.

These two episodes taught me that forgetfulness and remembrance work, like water, through currents, eddies, stagnant pools and sudden mysterious flows. Images come and go on the tides of memory, submerged, exposed, sometimes rubbed smooth or sprouting weird accretions. Ruth Sansom is dead now, and so are Vera and Judy Compton-Burnett. In the strange, compelling, demanding and absorbing hours I spent with them, we called spirits from the vasty deep, and they came.

Brian Harrison

The Dictionary Man

I was very happy as a tutorial fellow teaching modern history in an Oxford college for the 33 years between 1967 and 2000. It was a beautiful place in which to work; within very broad limits I could plan how I spent my time; I enjoyed remarkable freedom of speech; I had invigorating and regular discussions about interesting issues with intelligent young people, almost all of whom worked hard; I had ample time for research which I found very fulfilling; and I participated in the government of a small college, human in scale, with people I knew and liked. It seemed an ideal combination of scholarship and sociability, and for me the distinction between work and recreation which shapes the lives of most people did not exist. I was being paid for doing something I would have wanted to do anyway. By the 1990s the life was becoming less attractive because of fussily counter-productive government intervention (the acronyms TQA and RAE still send shudders down my spine) and empty 'mission statements', but a college tutor's life was still a good life, and I thought it would remain my life until I retired in 2004.

Then at 62, in a move that was totally unexpected even by me, let alone by others, I gave all this up for a life that was very different. From January 2000 to September 2004, as editor of the *Oxford Dictionary of National Biography*, my life came to resemble much more closely the lives that most people lead: I needed on working days to be in a particular place at specified times, my secretary needed to know my whereabouts when not there, I had a fixed allocation of leave, and I had an 'office' whose door usually needed to be open, and no college room in which to work uninterruptedly. My routines changed entirely: 'weekdays' and 'weekends' replaced 'term' and 'vacation', there were office parties, collectively signed birthday cards for the staff, coffee by the Xerox machine, and so on. There was at least as much intellectual stimulus as before, but greater reticence was required, given that the *Dictionary*'s authors and new biographical subjects had to be kept confidential until publication.

Why move, then? I didn't feel the slightest need for the 'new challenge' that seems to beset many people in late career: writing books has always been challenge enough for me. My move did of course reflect the importance of the *Dictionary* itself, and the need to ensure that it survived the sudden and tragic death from a heart attack at 58 of Colin Matthew (the biographer and editor of W. E. Gladstone) who had launched it in 1992. But there were also personal reasons growing out of the inquisitiveness that had always motivated me as an historian. I was intrigued to know what so different a life would be like and how I would cope with it. I had long admired Gladstone, especially for being so open to new ideas late in life: 'I have been a learner all my life', he said in a speech of 1890, 'and I am a learner still.' When deciding late in 1999 whether to accept the invitation of the University and the Oxford University Press to succeed Colin, I was attracted by the opportunity that working on the *Dictionary* would provide for finding out things, whereas as an experienced tutor I felt uncomfortable with the growing assumption that I already knew all the answers. It was because my lecturing and examining obligations made that assumption that they were alone among the duties before January 2000 that I really disliked; besides, I had lost faith in Oxford's examination system (scrupulously fair though it is, when viewed in its own terms) as an adequate or even sensible test of students' achievement.

As editor from 1985 to 1994 of the final volume in the *History of the University of Oxford* I had enjoyed helping to co-ordinate a group of people behind a shared research objective. So I relished the idea of heading what since 1992 has been in effect a research institute (and publishing initiative) within a university whose collegiate structure slants it unduly towards undergraduate teaching. Oxford's collective humanities research projects don't happen in the colleges, but in the Bodleian Library, the Oxford University Press and research institutes. As institutions, most Oxford colleges focus closely on undergraduate teaching, and on their ranking in the so-called 'Norrington table' of undergraduate examination results. The *Dictionary* is distant indeed from all this. In a building that at the project's peak in 2001–2 employed 29 research staff of the University, I alone held a college fellowship, and even that was because I had taught undergraduates for 33 years, and not in virtue of my new role. Working on the University's history had of course alerted me to the Oxford colleges' institutional distance from large research projects in the humanities, but there is nothing like personal experience for driving a point home.

So one of the *Dictionary*'s attractions for me was that in place of the college community for which I'd felt such strong affection, I acquired two new communities, one face-to-face and one 'virtual'. The first of these was the community of the University and Press employees who were producing it. I had contributed to the *DNB* supplement for 1986–90 and to *Missing Persons*, Christine Nicholls's supplementary volume to the entire dictionary published in 1993. Since 1992 I had corresponded with Colin Matthew about possible new subjects, and I wrote two short articles for him. I had even visited the *Dictionary*'s premises, 37A St Giles, twice. But not until 16 December 1999, when I first met its staff as Colin's successor, did I fully grasp the scale of the enterprise. As I stood in the entrance hall of what had once been a substantial early Victorian family house, introducing myself to the assembled company, 30 or 40 staff members filled the passageways and clustered up the sweeping curves of the staircase seemingly out of sight.

17 January 2000 was my first day at school, so to speak, and I arrived just in time to approve the 33,333rd article (on Amy Johnson) for publication. It was all rather bewildering at first. There were many new faces, many complex procedures and much bewildering terminology; people kept talking about TUD, STU, HAN, VIC and WEL, which I soon learned denoted some of the *Dictionary*'s research areas. Still more daunting was the continuously accumulating heap of articles to be approved. To ensure that the *Dictionary* was completed on time, each research editor was supposed each month to finish editing up to 50 of them. Human nature being what it is, the articles tended to arrive in the second half of the month, and my monthly total of at least 500 submitted for approval was intellectually and even physically challenging. Looking back now, we all sometimes wonder how we were able to do it. For three years, my life was dominated by this monthly cycle, with huge heaps of files, one for each article, to be transported to and from home in the evenings and at weekends during the end-of-month climacteric, followed by a short breather before the cycle resumed.

And yet through it all there was the excitement of building up a collective achievement, of making its components as good as they could be, and of ensuring that new biographical subjects were chosen fairly but imaginatively. Given that we could draw upon several hundred advisers, and given that Colin had already decided to include all people already in the *DNB*, my influence over selection was limited to adjudicating on marginal cases among the 13,500 newly included articles, but this left plenty of room for creativity. The later twentieth-century *DNB* supplements had broadened the policy on the types of person included and on how much could be said about their private lives; like Colin I had no hesitation in carrying forward the change. With one file per article and one file per contributor, shelves full of paper gradually spread out through the basements and cellars where Victorian wines had been stored and Victorian meals prepared, for behind the *Dictionary*'s computerized database a huge paper archive was steadily accumulating.

Amidst it all, two things I found reassuring: the smell of coffee brewing that pervaded the building from about 10 o'clock every weekday morning, and the photographs at the bottom of the stairs of the *Dictionary*'s first two editors, the bearded Leslie Stephen and the mustachioed Sidney Lee. If, somehow, they had survived the avalanche of paper, so could we.

But back to my two new communities. It was not long before 37A St Giles came to seem my natural home. With my research colleagues, in the University but not quite of it, I had many fascinating and wide-ranging discussions, not all of them historical or biographical. In one of them I was belatedly introduced to Bruckner. We often talked about periods of history that had been buried deeply in my mind beneath the layers of modern history tutorials I'd been giving since ceasing to be an undergraduate 40 years before. Then there were our more formal discussions about biography in the *DNB* seminar that was invented and organized by two of the research editors, and was held three times a term from 2002 to 2004. The research editors also taught me much about the technicalities of research, alert as they were to the full range of online resources now available. Nearly a tenth of the *Dictionary*'s 50,000 articles were written or revised in-house, together with important in-house enhancements to the rest. The research editors' diplomatic powers, their dedication to the project, their organizational grasp, and the sheer range of their expertise and resourcefulness at a relatively young age never ceased to impress me. They were thoroughly professional and self-effacing in their commitment to research, yet also (and necessarily) pragmatic. Somebody somewhere in the building always seemed to know the answer to any historical question – and that included football and pop music. Indeed, a downside of my life as editor was to see all but six of the research editors disperse as the project inevitably slimmed down once the *Dictionary*'s text was complete.

From my OUP colleagues – organizing the research and writing, designing the software and database, copy-editing, proof-reading, organizing data-capture, creating the *Dictionary*'s online version – I learned lessons very different but equally important: not just the formidable intellectual demands made by publishing a 60-volume reference work, but the sheer scale of its organizational complexities. Many of them were working for the *Dictionary* because they took a pride in it, and because they relished the special organizational and intellectual challenges which it presented. To facilitate and organize the research and writing, and to articulate editorial policy were not at all easy, and they required a very high-powered team. They also required what was sociologically a very interesting structure. With 10,000 contributors worldwide writing 50,000 articles in 12 years, this was inevitably complex, burgeoning with numerous codes and procedures, and buttressed by encyclopaedic in-house manuals. The *Dictionary*'s research material and administrative information were located from the start within a single computerized database, which made the project much easier to control. Furthermore, the database made the research material so readily available that the embryonic *Dictionary* itself became an increasingly valuable research tool: the earlier articles soon came to nourish the later. It was intriguing, too, to observe how the balance of work within the project shifted continuously as the *Dictionary* edged forward from research and writing to copy-editing and data-capture, to retrospective editing, to marketing and on to publicity. With creating the *Dictionary*, as with building a liner, the nature of the work and the balance of the workforce changed frequently. Or perhaps the analogy should be that of a ship being launched on a voyage of discovery: technological change in research and publishing since 1992 has been remarkable, and for us the unknown seemed always to be just over the horizon.

Not long after I arrived, we decided to hold things together by instituting a weekly meeting between editor, project director (Robert Faber) and research director (Liz Baigent). Practical and businesslike in mood, these meetings were at the same time enjoyable. Both Liz and Robert had been with the *Dictionary* from very early on, and here is my opportunity for paying tribute to them both. With a first-class degree in English, Robert had a superb grasp of the entire project, including its technical aspects, and combined this with a firm commitment to scholarly values and a remarkable capacity for getting people to work harmoniously with him. Liz, with a first-class degree and a doctorate in geography, enlivened my life with her splendid common sense, her invariably constructive approach to problems and her unfailing good humour; working with her was fun.

Like the *Oxford English Dictionary*, the *Oxford DNB* testifies to the compatibility, so often questioned within British universities, between entrepreneurial and scholarly values. The *Dictionary*'s commercial context was for me an attraction. I had served behind the counter as a teenager in my parents' shop, and then between national service and university I had again been behind a counter, this time in Selfridges' record department. However unfashionable it might be in late-twentieth-century academic life, a sneaking respect for the entrepreneur had been the outcome, and I welcomed the idea of ending my career in a more commercial climate. The *Dictionary* had originated, after all, with an entrepreneur, George Smith, publisher to (among others) the Brontës, and although charitable status makes the OUP's aims far broader than entrepreneurial, market disciplines are more salient there than in an Oxford college. Without those disciplines, the *Dictionary*'s content would have been narrower in scope, it would have been less responsive to outsiders, and its 60 volumes would never have been produced in 12 years. At no stage during my time as editor did I hear the OUP side of the project deploying commercial arguments to lower its scholarly standards: on the contrary, my OUP colleagues took pride in its reputation and integrity.

My second (and 'virtual') community was the community of contributors – 10,000 of them, worldwide. So large and scattered a community could hardly be close, but several devices drew it together. The editor signed all commissions and (in collaboration with the Research Director, Liz Baigent) sent out thank-you postcards when articles had been approved; newsletters were sent out three times a year; and once a month I sent out a website message on the project's progress. I never ceased to feel an affinity with the contributors; I had after all only recently been one of them, and throughout my time as editor I retained strong feelings of obligation towards them. I had feared at first that some contributors would embrace the academic fashions that make for deliberate obscurity and pretentiousness, whereas a work of reference must aim always for clarity and conciseness; yet the devotees of such fashions must have weeded themselves out because this never became a problem. For Leslie Stephen, punctuality and consideration were 'the two cardinal virtues of a contributor', and from all but a handful of contributors that is what we encountered. From many I received postcards, notes of encouragement, and even the occasional lunch in a London club.

Of course it wasn't all plain sailing. Succeeding an able predecessor can be awkward. I hadn't been editor six months before a lively North Oxford teenager came to us for work experience and asked me, no doubt echoing some adult conversation he'd overheard, 'Do you think you're living in Colin Matthew's shadow?' Out of the mouths of babes . . . It was a shrewd and honest question, but for at least three reasons it was wide of the mark. First, I received staunch backing from beginning to end from Colin's widow and from other members of his family. Second, this wasn't the first time I'd had a distinguished predecessor: since 1967 in my college I had been teaching history in the post previously held by the historian Michael Brock. After playing a central role within the college, he became prominent in university affairs as Bursar of one Oxford college and then as Warden of another. Third, I found it easy to fit in to the mould that Colin had established for the *Dictionary* because my view of history closely resembled his. Whereas he had begun largely as a political historian and had opened out towards social history, I had begun as a social historian and had opened out towards political history; we met somewhere in the middle, and with none of his significant decisions about the *Dictionary* did I disagree.

In my book *Peaceable Kingdom* I claimed that 'biography is procedurally the easiest of the historian's activities'. I think I meant that although biography is in principle as difficult as any other approach to history, it is in practice relatively easy for a biographer to reach a minimum level of competence: the book's shape, sources and theme are all relatively pre-determined. Yet it wasn't long before I moved sufficiently towards biography as a mode of historical writing to publish in 1987 a study of 16 inter-war feminists in my *Prudent Revolutionaries*. Then on arriving at the *Dictionary*, I began to interest myself in its history, and in writing 29 articles for it I was alerted to the important distinction between what one might call 'tombstone' and 'capsule' biography. My reservations about the first remain, but I'm much more alert now to the merits of the second, and to the challenges it presents. It requires a conciseness, a confronting of priorities and a comparative frame of reference which are not at all easily attained. And when the capsule biography of an individual is combined with 50,000 others, many of them relatively obscure, and when the articles include 'group biographies' (of families, business firms and cultural groups), and when they are all powerfully searchable online – the social historian's grumbles about biography's limitations as an approach to historical study dissolve into nothingness.

Sara Wheeler

Polar Gap

As a rookie biographer I struggle hardest with problems created by the frailties of evidence, putting style aside (if only one could). The issue first revealed itself when I was writing the life of Apsley Cherry-Garrard, one of Captain Scott's men and the author of the 1922 polar classic *The Worst Journey in the World*. For Cherry's last restless decades I relied on the testimony of his widow, Angela, a woman in her 80s who, like most of us, could not reliably recall what happened half a century ago (though she thought she could: she saw it so clearly). During the Second World War she and Cherry lived near Baker Street in London in a sixth-floor flat beneath Bertrand Russell, his third wife Patricia Spence, known as 'Peter', and their schoolboy son Conrad. Angela told me how Cherry, lost in the fug of a black depression, had become so enraged by the sound of one of the Russells playing the piano that he despatched his wife upstairs to ask them to desist. This was an intimidating task: a fresh young woman from the provinces issuing orders to one of the towering intellects of the Western world. When she havered, Cherry persisted innocently, 'I'd do it for you', as if that situation would have been remotely comparable – he was a famous landed gent of 60. Anyway, I wrote to Conrad, by then the fifth Earl, to ask if he remembered his grumpy neighbour. He did, and offered perceptive comments from a mature perspective. 'But,' he concluded the letter, 'we never owned a piano.'

In the absence of a primary source (a delivery note from the piano company), what is one to do? Had Conrad Russell not replied to my enquiry, the temptation to deploy unreliable memory as if it were fact would have been irresistible.

Even when there is a primary source, it has the irritating habit of conflicting with another primary source. What do you do when you reach an unbridgeable abyss of ignorance between two apparently contradictory bits of evidence? I was piecing together the life of Edith, the youngest of Cherry's five sisters. Born in 1896, Edith was always a shadowy figure in the family saga. A physically weak child, she was designated an invalid in the Victorian manner and confined to a wicker spinal chair. She features in photographs parked under far-off chestnut trees with her nurse while her siblings rampage about in the foreground. Nothing further is heard of Evelyn until 1923, when she appears in a magazine standing alone on top of the Matterhorn in stout boots and a good tweed skirt. I had material about the beginning of her life, and material about the end: yet the one was so different from the other that it seemed impossible to trace a route between the two.

A third serious problem was queuing up for attention. It emerged that the information I did have was disastrously unevenly spaced. Most biographers are familiar with the agony of the declining decades – that yawning phase about which one longs to write, 'And so the years passed'. In my case the problem was attenuated, as Cherry's Antarctic expedition – the emotional focus of his life – reached its dismal conclusion when he was 26. I still had 47 years to go; years in which not much happened, barring a couple of world wars. Never again. Curiously, my next and current subject, Denys Finch Hatton, died at the age of 44 . . . Onward to Keats and Chatterton? In the case of Finch Hatton, the English aristocrat and East African white hunter whom Karen Blixen loved, there is almost no primary material. He did not keep diaries, fewer than a dozen of his letters survive and as he pranged his plane into the Ngong hills in 1931 hardly anyone alive remembers him. This was my fourth problem, and I'm finding it the most challenging of the lot. My only comfort is the knowledge that an absence of meaty sources is not necessarily a handicap. Hilary Spurling wrote her brilliant second volume on Ivy Compton-Burnett out of 50 years of postcards saying 'Please come to tea.'

How is one to fill the gaps? You can't make it up; you can't invite the reader to take his choice; you can't do nothing. I battle daily not to gratify the biographer's need to impose coherence (seeing so clearly that in my own life there is none). All I have usefully concluded so far is that the only solution is to work out a way of conjuring the past without resorting to fiction. But there's another thing about material, though, more important than all the above. It's to do with its quality. Biographies tend to fail if they take a doggedly factual approach that ignores the gloopy layers of emotional and imaginative experience that make us human. They take wing only when they are released from the tyranny of the card index. It might be a truism to say that the reader doesn't need all the facts, he needs the fertile ones; but if so it is a truism with which many life writers appear to disagree. As Sir Thomas North, the sixteenth-century translator of Plutarch's *Lives*, put it, 'What signifies it to us, how many battles Alexander the Great fought; it were more to the purpose to say how often he was drunk.' The subject's inner life is the life we care about. (Now I come to think of it, a gap in the material is a useful metaphor for the inner life.) But similarly, biographies are not, as John Updike contended, 'just novels with indexes'. The best ones combine scholarship with imaginative storytelling (Michael Holroyd's *Augustus John*, David Cecil's *Lord M*, about Melbourne).

I'm sorry to go on about metaphors but it seems to me that the elusive, unreliable and flame-like nature of primary material is not unlike the human spirit: capricious, contradictory and inconclusive. The gaps represent the fundamental, immutable isolation of one human being from another. Whom do we really know? But seeing through a glass darkly is still seeing. Or is it?

Claire Tomalin

Starting Over

Claire Tomalin is one of Britain's finest biographers. Her last biography, Samuel Pepys: The Unequalled Self, *was awarded the Whitbread Book of the Year Prize for 2002. She is currently in the early stages of writing a life of the poet and novelist Thomas Hardy. Her new home, just outside Richmond in Surrey, seems like some twenty-first century version of a Hardyesque rural idyll, surrounded by fields of cows and disused milking sheds, its tranquillity punctuated only by the roar of passing traffic.*

Describe your state of mind on finishing Pepys.
The book had been such a huge effort – stepping into a new century and trying to inhabit it, not to mention one and a quarter million words of Pepys's diary which I must have re-read four times (and I still get surprises when I look at it now). I went into the project with terrific enthusiasm, but for much of the time while I was trying to write it, I was in absolute despondency. And after I'd finished it, no one was fantastically keen on it. They were polite, but it didn't capture Michael's [her husband Michael Frayn] fancy much. I actually thought it would drop like a stone.

I'd had a rather nasty shock halfway through of another book on Pepys coming out, which I hadn't known about at all, but I wasn't too worried about it when I looked at it – it wasn't what I was trying to do. So when I got my first good review from Craig Brown in the *Mail on Sunday* – and it was probably the best review I have ever had – I was completely knocked sideways. There were some 'iffy' reviews, but the impression became that it was getting a very good reception, and it really took off.

But I was extremely reluctant to start on something else. We were moving house after 40 years, my father was dying, and the political situation (I had finished *Pepys* on 9/11) weren't encouragements to start on something else.

Also, I felt deeply depressed when Pepys died. I had grown so attached to him, despite his defects of character. I think the older you get as a biographer, the less you are prepared to tick anyone off for their failings. You have lived your own life and you are somehow more accepting of other people's flaws.

What attracted you to Hardy as a biographical subject?
I'd actually had a contract to write about Hardy years ago, which I gave up. Finally, last year, I agreed to do it. I had wanted to stay in the seventeenth century as it seems so close to us, whereas the nineteenth century is so distant. Indeed, all the work I have been doing on Hardy has rather confirmed this in my mind. When you return to the nineteenth century, it's as if a great grey blanket has fallen on everybody. I have had quite a long break, and even now I'm working incredibly hard on the new garden. But I like to think of myself as some sort of agricultural labourer – which is very good preparation for writing about Hardy!

Hardy is somebody I read when I was young. I read his novels first but then soon turned to his poetry. He is one of the great English poets. Look at his extraordinary output and extraordinary range. Philip Larkin made a telling remark about him, saying that there was a little spinal cord of thought going through all Hardy's poems, and almost every poem has a little tune of his own. That's absolutely right. Hardy forges this language – it's very easy to parody and has been well parodied often. It doesn't sound like ordinary language and yet he makes out of it something absolutely true when talking about human experience.

What you look for when you are thinking about a biography are the stories in somebody's life. The first story I thought of in Hardy's case was of a man who thought he was a poet, and wasn't allowed to be a poet because he had to earn his living. So he wrote novels, inventing his fictional world of Wessex. There are some very great works, though they're quite uneven and he himself felt that he hadn't given them the finish and attention that he perhaps should have done, which I think is right. Many people have condescended to Hardy the novel writer, starting with Henry James and going on to F. R. Leavis. As he progressed, though, he produced two remarkable novels, *Tess of the D'Urbevilles* and *Jude the Obscure*. Then there's this extraordinary apotheosis on the death of his first wife Emma, and he writes a series of great poems in his 70s. That's a great story, and I'm especially interested in old men (I was fascinated by Pepys in his old age), perhaps because of my father dying at 98.

Another strong strand of narrative revolves around this original, brilliant boy born into almost the lowest level of English society in 1840, at a time when your level in society had never been so important. He was denied education, denied social status, denied opportunity, and spent all his life struggling, never really gaining social confidence. And then when he is taken up and acknowledged by literary men in London and asked to join their clubs, and when society hostesses flatter him, he's so vulnerable.

Hardy's mother and grandmothers were women who were free as young women, and became pregnant before they were married. Dorset rural life then was very unsophisticated. But then you get this extraordinary development. Jemima Hardy has four children – with Hardy the eldest – yet none of them have any sort of sexual freedom. Hardy marries very late in defiance of his mother. Before that we have these obscure years of his young manhood: he talks afterwards of how deeply depressed he was during those years, and of how he used to go dancing in London. He seems to have been involved with lots of girls, but never to have found lasting fulfilment. Then he meets Emma, and marries her out of love. It's terribly bad luck that they don't have children. If they had, Emma would have absorbed herself in her family and the strains upon them would have been different. Earlier biographers, especially Robert Gittings, have pointed out how extremely badly Hardy behaved. But writers protect themselves ferociously. So the story of that marriage, and of how it goes wrong, is also fascinating.

You have been recently to see the manuscript of Jude *at the Fitzwilliam Museum in Cambridge. What insights did you gain from this?*
Yes, Hardy's friend Sidney Cockerell, the Director of the Museum, persuaded Hardy to give his manuscripts to the Fitzwilliam, and another friend had some of them bound. As a gift for doing this, Hardy allowed him to keep the manuscript of one novel, though he was adamant that on the friend's death, it shouldn't be allowed to go to America – in the end it went to Dublin.

There have been scholarly accounts of the manuscript of *Jude*, so I didn't learn much that was new, except that 50 pages of it are missing, and they're all the most contentious pages, and I'd like to know at what point those pages were removed, and by whom. One of the fascinating things about the manuscript – it's a fair copy, not a rough draft – is that in the original version Hardy made Sue Brideshead, Jude's cousin, into an orphan who was adopted by the Provost of an Oxford college, and brought up in Oxford. He doesn't do anything with that. Also the names are changed all the time. Jude starts as Jack, for instance. And there's another ghastly change from manuscript to novel. In the published version, the eldest child, 'Old Father Time', son of Jude and Arabella, hangs the two babies and himself. But in the manuscript he only hangs one other child; and apparently at proof stage, Hardy adds a little girl, makes Sue have a little daughter, which slightly makes one gag, doesn't it? I mean, to make it worse in that way. It would have been quite bad enough for him just to hang himself.

There seems among many biographers to be a divide between those who claim great intimacy with their subject, and those who are more coolly dispassionate. Where do you place yourself?
I think the impulse behind writing biography is the same as the impulse that lies behind most writing. It's the ability to see stories, to tell stories, as I was saying before. You have to have that driving force. Of course, it's fatuous to claim intimacy with somebody who has been dead for a long time, and with whom you have never been intimate. What I do at the moment mostly is think. I've re-read all the novels and the poems, read other biographies. With Hardy there's the same problem as there was with Jane Austen. There's a huge mass of academic material which I have to acquaint myself with, even though some of it, to put it mildly, seems far-fetched. But there's some superb critical writing on the poetry. Thom Gunn's essay, for instance, on the qualities of the ballad in Hardy's verse: the lack of personality and of narrative coherence, the use of a voice, and you're not quite sure whose voice is speaking.

How do you organize your research?
I'm in that agreeable phase of preparing myself to write. Organizationally, it's utterly different from Pepys. Hardy's letters are, more or less, all published; Pepys's weren't. I don't expect to discover anything new, rather to see Hardy from a new perspec-

tive. I've hugely admired Gittings's books, but there's something not quite right about his second volume. Millgate's book [*Thomas Hardy*, 1982] is the definitive research biography, while Martin Seymour-Smith's [*Hardy*, 1994] is preposterous – and yet it is fuelled by love and passion.

I've got endless files containing things like a chronology, which is very important, and a cast list. I'm also very interested in context. I'd like to open up part of the book for a comparison between Hardy and Kilvert, who was contemporary, from a different social background, but who shared many of the same concerns about rural life. Joseph Arch, an itinerant agricultural labourer who was instrumental in forming the first Agricultural Labourers' Union, and who did more than any other man of his time to improve the conditions of agricultural workers, is another significant point of comparison. But who knows how it will turn out? When I started my book on Dickens's mistress Ellen Ternan [*The Invisible Woman*, 1991], I was originally going to tell the entire story through her son's eyes. Then I changed my mind.

Mark Bostridge

Ipplepen 269

In the summer of 1986 I was almost broke and in desperate need of gainful employment. The previous year I had worked as a research assistant to the politician Shirley Williams, then President of the SDP. My main task had been gathering material for a book she was writing about the terrifying levels of rising unemployment in Thatcher's Britain. While Shirley dashed around the country, addressing the party faithful, I sat in front of an early model Apple Macintosh computer in her London flat, unravelling and typing chapters from the handwritten scripts on long yellow notepads that she occasionally flung at me in her rush to the station. I also found myself inveigled into a fair amount of hoovering and fetching and carrying of dry cleaning, though I rather appreciated the feminist role-reversal implicit in these activities. What I dreaded were my days at party headquarters in Cowley Street, avoiding the brooding Heathcliffian figure of Dr David Owen, the SDP's man of destiny, who was said to be more than a little concerned about the inefficiencies of Shirley's office.

But all this had come to an end with the publication of her book. It was called *A Job To Live* – an appropriate title in view of the situation in which I now found myself. For a while I drifted through an unsatisfactory series of temporary jobs. Then I hit on an idea that had been lodged in the back of my mind for some time: I would write a short book about Shirley's mother, Vera Brittain, feminist and pacifist, and author of the classic woman's memoir of the First World War, *Testament of Youth*.

I had read *Testament of Youth* several years earlier as an undergraduate at Oxford, and had immediately become obsessed with it. It opened my eyes to the suffering of the combatants and non-combatants of the Great War in a way that nothing else had done, and made me understand the cataclysmic impact of the war on a young woman from an ordinary middle-class background not dissimilar to my own. It is also a book that is suffused, at least in its early sections, with the romance of Oxford together with an excitement about the intellectual opportunities offered by the University, which at that time I certainly shared.

Another, more personal reason for my interest was that two of my close friends, one from school, the other from university, were Vera Brittain's grandson and granddaughter. Some time later, after I had been appointed as Brittain's biographer, I read Penelope Lively's fine novel, *According To Mark*, and relished the parallels in the plot to my own position in real life. Mark Lamming is writing the biography of Gilbert Strong, a literary figure between the wars, described as on the fringes of the Bloomsbury Group. In the course of his researches, Mark meets his subject's granddaughter Carrie, and although he initially suffers from 'chronological irritation' because his version of events does not always accord with Carrie's memories of her grandfather, he soon falls in love with her, leading to momentous consequences for the writing of his book. I hadn't fallen in love with my subject's granddaughter, nor she with me, but I had experienced something of the same flicker of recognition that is present in the novel, when the biographer notices certain of Gilbert Strong's personality traits replicated in a later generation.

One of the bonuses of working for Shirley Williams was the chance, in odd moments free from all the frantic politicking, to talk to her about her mother, to look at old family photographs, and at the William Rothenstein portrait of Brittain, painted at the height of the Second World War, at a time when her courageously defiant pacifist views were jeopardizing her literary standing, and isolating her from her friends. There were other, more poignant relics from the past lying around the flat, like the inky school copy of the Liddell and Scott that had belonged to Vera's adored younger brother Edward, one of the central figures of *Testament of Youth*. Edward had left Uppingham School in that fateful summer of 1914 and had responded eagerly to the call of King and Country, serving with distinction on the Western Front before being posted to Italy where he was killed on the Asiago Plateau in the final months of the war.

Shirley was very supportive of my idea for a brief study of Vera Brittain that would set her life and writing in a proper historical context. At Oxford I had been awarded the history prize that, some 60 years earlier, Shirley's father, the political scientist George Catlin, had also won. Although she isn't a superstitious person, I think that this coincidence provided enough of an encouragement to her to believe that I was in some way meant to write about her mother. When she learned of my plan, Shirley immediately wrote to Carmen Callil, recommending both my prospective book and me. As one of the founders of Virago, Carmen had republished *Testament of Youth* in the late 1970s with enormous flair and success, establishing the book, after a long period of neglect, as part of the canon of writing about the First World War, and pushing it once again to the top of the bestseller lists.

Carmen replied from her office at Chatto & Windus where she had recently been appointed managing director. She wasn't keen on a short book, but she had another suggestion to put to Shirley: as the authorized biography of Vera Brittain by Brittain's friend and literary executor Paul Berry was some years overdue, why didn't I step in as co-author to help him finish it?

I knew something about Paul Berry, and had met him briefly the previous summer. Born in 1919, the eighth of ten children of a Midlands farming family, he was a remote cousin on his mother's side of Vera Brittain's great friend, the Yorkshire novelist and reformer Winifred Holtby. Paul had introduced himself to Brittain at a Food Relief Rally in Trafalgar Square at which she was speaking in the summer of 1942. 'Charming young man', she noted in her diary, 'with a distant look of Winifred. He is in a bomb-disposal squad at Acton – [a] compromise bet.[ween] being a C.O. [conscientious objector] & being in the army.' On an impulse she invited him back to supper with her, and he stayed until after ten.

This was the beginning of a friendship that would last almost 28 years, right up to Brittain's death in March 1970. For Paul, it was undoubtedly the single most important relationship of his life. He was drawn to her, partly out of respect for his own mother whose 'sanctity and strong matriarchal influence' had, he claimed, made him a feminist; and also because he saw the vulnerability in Vera Brittain's character, perceiving under the rather flinty surface a sweeter and softer side to her personality that rarely emerged in public. This made him protective of her – in death as well as in life – and led him to imbue their relationship with an almost romantic aura. One of the first gifts he sent her was a box of violets, in direct imitation of those she had once received from her fiancé Roland Leighton, fatally wounded at the Front at Christmas 1915.

But it was far from being a one-sided friendship. Shy and withdrawn, Vera Brittain found intimacy difficult. At the time of first meeting Paul Berry, she was suffering from the devastating blow of being prevented by the government from visiting her son and daughter who had been evacuated to the United States. In Paul she discovered a young man who shared many of her views – he remained a lifelong pacifist – and who in some ways fulfilled the role of surrogate son. In 1944, when she was writing her novel

Born 1925 she drew closely on his experiences as a bomb-disposal soldier for the character of the hero Adrian, who became a composite of Paul, and Brittain's son John.

For many years Paul had worked as a teacher of secretarial skills, eventually becoming a Senior Lecturer at Kingsway-Princeton College for Further Education, from which he had retired in 1981. His major ambition, though, had always been to be a writer, and he had published two short books, one in collaboration with another author. But the book he most wanted to write had come close to defeating him. Originally intending, at Brittain's request, to complete her third volume of autobiography, left unfinished at her death, he subsequently conceived the idea of a memoir, and then, as Vera Brittain's reputation revived, of a fully-fledged biography. He had always experienced difficulty writing – though he was an accomplished and indefatigable correspondent – and found himself, understandably, floundering in the morass of material which Brittain had left behind, much of it preserved at McMaster University in Ontario which had purchased the vast Brittain archive in 1971. 'It's the one thing I want to do before I go on my way – and do really well', he wrote to Carmen Callil, 'and it's soul-destroying finding it so terribly difficult.'

In the years to come, I often reflected on what seemed to me an extraordinary (though entirely characteristic) loyalty on Shirley's part towards Paul's overriding desire to be her mother's authorized biographer, often against a chorus of hostile voices from feminist academics in North America who resented the ban on the use of unpublished material while Paul was writing his book. Yet, as one of Shirley's oldest friends put it to me, a more complicated mixture of motives was probably involved. While she clearly felt a sense of obligation towards him, she may also have believed that she could rely on Paul to produce a respectful biography of her mother that wouldn't dwell on the more controversial aspects of Vera Brittain's private life: her 'semi-detached' marriage, ultimately a happy one, but for many years a source of conflict and estrangement; her great friendship with Winifred Holtby, for so long a subject of the innuendo and rumour that portrayed it as a lesbian love affair; and, in her final years, Brittain's sadly deteriorating relationship with her son John. As I was soon to learn, another of Paul's problems was that he was constantly torn between his desire on the one hand to protect Brittain's reputation, and on the other to be as honest as he could about her faults as well as her virtues.

Our first professional encounter at Chatto's offices in William IV Street was hardly auspicious. Having negotiated the tricky metal grille of the old-fashioned lift, I arrived in Carmen's room, its walls a virulent shade of yellow, to find her enquiring after Paul's cat Bobbitt and complaining about the state of the office lavatories. She was smoking furiously, and as she turned her head, shafts of sunlight sent off rays of iridescent colour from her hair, Titian red, then rich aubergine. Paul regarded me with watery blue eyes, peeping over the folds of a large white hand-kerchief, a study in suspicion.

Carmen requested that he invite me to his home in West Sussex to look at the material he had collected. When he demurred, citing the excuse of his large family and a sick friend, she suddenly transformed from benign autocrat to belligerent dictator: *he would co-operate and make everything available to me or else the book that meant so much to him might never appear.*

Paul had accumulated a massive Brittain archive of his own, housed in a cobwebby study at the top of one of the five tiny cottages that had been knocked together in a higgledy-piggledy fashion to construct a home. Here were hundreds of photocopies from McMaster, countless pages of Brittain manuscripts and newscuttings retrieved from her London flat after her death or subsequently donated to him, letters of reminiscence from people who had known Vera Brittain, and both sides of more than a quarter-of-a-century's correspondence between Paul and Brittain herself. Although I was to make trips to McMaster and to the Winifred Holtby Archive at Hull, as well as to many other collections, the discoveries that surprised me most were often those that I found under a pile of decaying newsprint on Paul's study floor.

It quickly became apparent that there was no book to finish, and that little of what Paul had written was usable. He possessed a striking turn of phrase, which I often adopted, but was unable to see the wood for the trees, or to organize the material in a way that would produce a coherent narrative. Initially, his argument that we shouldn't write about Brittain's First World War experiences because they were so well known drove me to distraction. I would return from my visits to Sussex, my briefcase full to overflowing with files of fascinating material to work on, but with a sinking feeling about the prospect of ever being able to weld together our widely differing approaches to our subject.

With Paul himself I began to enjoy a real friendship, even though we were separated in age by more than 40 years. Our relationship was still tempered by his natural suspicion and stubbornness, and on my part, by over-eagerness to probe deeply into every aspect of Vera Brittain's life and career. But I appreciated his inexhaustible generosity ('There are no pockets in the shrouds', he would say as he slipped me a £20 note) and recognized the quiet integrity that struck everyone who knew him. My visits to the picturesque little cottages with their lush surrounding garden, nestling by a river, became more frequent; but, as the years passed, our roles reversed. I was writing more and more, while he increasingly assumed an editorial responsibility, poring over my typescripts and scrutinizing them for grammatical error, infelicities of expression, and factual mistakes. I knew how desperate he was that the book should appear, but my progress was interrupted by my spells of employment at the BBC when I barely had time to write at all. Today, reading the letters I wrote to Paul during this period, I am filled with shame at their constant note of prevarication and delay. Year after year I promise him that the completion of the book is imminent. By the beginning of 1994 he was seriously ill and had begun to put real pressure on me: he might not live to see the publication of the book. That summer I finally finished it, but working with a sympathetic copy-editor persuaded me that it could be improved still further, and in the last four months of that year I drastically rewrote it. Paul couldn't disguise his anger. Although we were reconciled long before his death in 1999, there was always the unspoken accusation between us, that I had taken his book away from him. What he can't have failed to recognize is that he had given the biography something infinitely precious: that stamp of authenticity that can only come from close personal knowledge of the biographer's subject.

*   *   *

For more than 30 years Paul had shared his life with the distinguished potter Ray Marshall, and after Marshall's death in 1986, he had spent his final decade in a happy companionship with the artist Eric Leazell. Paul wasn't tortured or defensive about his homosexuality, though he was secretive about it, understandably given that he had grown to maturity in pre-Wolfenden days. And his sexuality had perhaps led him to examine in some detail the character of Vera Brittain's brother Edward, and the circumstances surrounding his death in 1918. On one of my first visits to see him, Paul had shown me the letters relating to this episode that he had uncovered at McMaster.

Edward is a tragic subsidiary character in Vera Brittain's story. He – along with his Uppingham friends, Roland Leighton and Victor Richardson – exemplified the volunteer spirit of the public schoolboys who rushed to enlist on the declaration of war in 1914. When Edward was gazetted to a battalion of the Sherwood Foresters, he proudly sent a photograph of himself in 'the King's uniform' to his old governess. 'What greater honour', she replied, 'could any man have at such a time as this in our history!'

Edward became a family hero, awarded the Military Cross 'for conspicuous gallantry and leadership during an attack' on the first day of the Somme. However, the experience of crawling back in great pain to the safety of the British trenches through the dead and wounded, with corpses already turning yellow and green, had eroded his youthful idealism. 'You have no idea how bitter life is at times', he wrote to Vera when he was back in the mud and cold of the Ypres Salient.

By the autumn of 1917, when he was posted to Italy, he had suffered the deaths of his old friends, Roland and Victor, and of another close friend from his former battalion, Geoffrey Thurlow, all fatally wounded or killed on the Western Front, and these had intensified Edward's long-held premonition that he too would be killed. His family's hopes, though, that he would survive the war were boosted now that Edward was in the relatively quiescent Italian Front high in the Alps above Vicenza.

But those hopes were shattered on 22 June 1918 by the arrival of a telegram informing the Brittains that Edward had been killed on the Asiago Plateau while leading a counter-offensive against an Austrian attack. The absence of any firm details about Edward's death led Vera Brittain to contact his commanding officer, who was in hospital in London, recovering from the injuries he had sustained in the same battle. For several months she pursued him relentlessly, convinced that he knew far more about Edward's part in the action than he was prepared to tell. However, it was all to no avail, and Edward's final hours remained cloaked in mystery.

This much was recounted in *Testament of Youth* and confirmed by the contemporary documents. But the McMaster material added an intriguing new twist to the plot. In 1934, 15 years after Edward's death, and following the publication of *Testament of Youth*, the commanding officer had written to Vera, out of the blue, to confess that, as she had intuitively believed in 1918, he had withheld certain facts of a personal nature about Edward's death. Even at that distance in time he could not bring himself to write about it, but he suggested that if she still wished to have the information they could meet for a talk.

But what were these facts of a personal nature that the commanding officer couldn't write down? Here, tantalizingly, the written sources went blank. From subsequent letters among the Brittain papers, it was clear that a meeting had taken place, but of their conversation, no record appeared to survive.

Paul pointed to the evidence of Vera Brittain's third novel, an ambitious feminist epic, *Honourable Estate*, which Brittain had written after *Testament of Youth*, but which had failed to repeat the runaway success of her autobiography. The book had been published in 1936, a couple of years after the commanding officer had met for his conversation with Brittain. Each of Vera Brittain's five novels is a *roman à clef* in which identifiable persons from real life are presented as thinly disguised fictional characters; even so, the plotline of *Honourable Estate* seemed almost too dramatic to be true. In the novel Richard Alleyndene, the brother of the heroine Ruth, goes into the Gallipoli campaign seeking to be killed in order to avoid a court martial for homosexuality. 'I can't confront

Father and Mother with the fact that their son is what they would call vicious and immoral,' he tells her in a farewell letter, 'instead of a virtuous patriotic hero.'

Staying at about this time with George Catlin's second wife, Delinda, who, since his death in 1979, had lived in Vera Brittain's cottage in the New Forest, I made a small but satisfying find. At the bottom of the bathroom cupboard, covered in thick dust, was a head and shoulders portrait of Edward, wearing his MC. The canvas had holes in it and the paint was peeling, but I could make out his sad smile and dignified bearing. I took it downstairs to show Delinda who was nursing her lunchtime gin and tonic.

Delinda was the consummate hostess, having in the distant past been the manager of several upmarket hotels. In every way imaginable she was the polar opposite of her distinguished predecessor, Vera Brittain, who had wasted no time on culinary matters, being barely able to boil an egg. Among other things, Delinda rejected books, feminism, the Labour Party, or anything else that smacked of intellectualism. She verbalized her thoughts in a down-to-earth, call-a-spade-a-spade fashion that emanated from her Newcastle-upon-Tyne roots. 'Dahling,' she drawled after taking one look at the painting, 'of course, everyone knows he was a pansy.'

Like Chinese whispers, other unsubstantiated rumours swirled around Edward's name. An academic researching the novelist Joyce Cary reported that Cary's brother-in-law Heneage Ogilvy, who had been a surgeon at Asiago in 1918, had known something about a court martial in connection with Edward. But having been unable to gain access to the official records held by the Ministry of Defence, which at the time were embargoed, I tried to think of other leads to follow.

Another obvious starting point was Edward's commanding officer. In Richmond Reference Library, near where I lived, I located the entry for Brigadier C. E. Hudson in the 1951–60 volume of *Who Was Who*. This revealed that Hudson had remained in the army after the war, becoming Chief Instructor at the Royal Military College at Sandhurst, and eventually, during the Second World War, ADC to George VI. He had had one son, had died in 1959, and his address had been Denbury Manor in Devon. The book even helpfully gave his telephone number – Ipplepen 269 – though since he was dead, that seemed, to put it mildly, somewhat superfluous.

Ipplepen 269. Over the next few weeks the number seared itself on my brain. I rang British Telecom on several occasions to see whether an operator could convert the number into its modern-day equivalent, but the harder I tried to explain what I was attempting to do, the more convoluted the muddle both the operator and I seemed to get into. Finally, I had almost decided to travel down to Devon to see if the house was still standing, when I had another idea. Hudson had been at Sherborne School. Wasn't there a chance that he might have sent his son there too? Feeling slightly fainthearted now, I rang the Sherborne Old Boys Association, spoke to its secretary, and explained my predicament. He was doubtful about any prospect of success, but promised to do what he could. A week later, having forgotten all about it, I was just sitting down to dinner when I received a call from the secretary. My guess had been right. Hudson had sent his son to Sherborne, and he gave me the son's telephone number.

I nervously rang the number. A woman answered, identifying herself as the son's wife. I embarked on my story, but she stopped me after several sentences.

'Good gracious,' she said; 'we've been expecting someone to contact us about this for years.'

Hudson's son couldn't have been more open and helpful. As I struggled to contain my excitement, he told me that his father had recorded all that he knew about Edward's death in his unpublished memoirs and that, of course, I was welcome to read them. 'What a wonderful coup tracking down Hudson's son,' Paul wrote to me when he heard the news; 'that really is *something*.' Looking at Paul's letter as I write this, I see that it is dated 15 June 1989, the seventy-first anniversary of Edward's death.

However, Hudson's son did make one proviso. I must first obtain Shirley Williams's permission before he could allow me to see the contents of his father's book. This proved to be much more of an obstacle than I anticipated.

Shirley had been remarkably generous in answering my enquiries, and in allowing me access to material in her possession. But in this one instance she at first expressed her outright refusal to co-operate. She wasn't at all sure that I should be allowed to delve further into the murky secrets of her uncle's past. Hudson's memoirs, she said, might only reveal Edward to have been involved in a love affair condemned by the bigotry and hypocrisy of the time; or they might show it be something discreditable, like the seduction of a young recruit by Edward as his junior officer.

I remember my feelings at the time as being ones of anger and frustration during which I tried to enlist the support of other members of Vera Brittain's family to speak up for my cause. 'I'm really grieved and sad that you're having so much trouble from Shirley over the Hudson book', Paul wrote. 'We – and especially you – have far too much to do and worry about without this sort of spanner in the works . . . I'm sure you've thought of all the arguments you can use. I do hope that you can get [Hudson's son] on your side although I have a hunch that opposition only makes Shirley more determined.'

Looking back now, though, I see these events as much less clear-cut. As a biographer I had got hold of a good story which I wanted to milk for all its worth. It was as if I had been overcome by a kind of narrative greed, which paid no attention to the sensitivities of those more directly affected by possible revelations than I was. Much has been made of the ways in which a family can manipulate and bully an authorized biographer; too little has been said of the biographer's ruthlessness in sometimes wilfully ignoring the family's point of view.

In the event, it was Hudson's son who came to my rescue. He was surprised by Shirley's reaction, and had in any case only requested her permission as a courtesy to her. He was far more concerned with setting the record straight regarding the reputation of his father who, he believed, had been 'grossly traduced' by what Vera Brittain had written of him in *Testament of Youth*. After a couple of weeks, which I spent on tenterhooks, waiting for a final answer, we reached a compromise: Shirley would read the memoirs first in order to decide whether I should be allowed to see them.

So on a boiling hot July day, I made my way to Brooks's Club in St James's to meet Hudson's son. Twenty minutes before my arrival, Shirley had departed after agreeing that I could read his father's book. In the staid, slightly incongruous atmosphere of a gentlemen's club, the shocking circumstances of Edward Brittain's death unfolded before my eyes.

*   *   *

On 12 June 1918, Edward's commanding officer, Colonel Hudson, had received a communication from the Provost Marshal, the head of the Military Police, informing him that a letter written by one of his officers while on leave to another officer in the battalion, had been intercepted and censored at the Base. The contents of this letter made it plain that the two officers were involved in homosexual relations with men in their company. The more senior of the two was Captain Brittain. Hudson was instructed that he was to avoid letting the officers concerned know that they were under investigation.

But, according to Hudson's later account, he was inclined to treat Edward more sympathetically, and on 14 June – the day before the Austrian offensive on the Asiago Plateau commenced – he had a conversation with Edward in which he gave him a warning. 'I did not realize that letters written out here were censored at the Base.' Edward turned white and made no comment. But it was clear that he had understood.

Edward was the only officer killed on 15 June. After the battle, Hudson had reached the terrible conclusion that, faced in all likelihood with the prospect of a court martial when they came out of the line, imprisonment, and the subsequent disgrace that would ensue, Edward had either shot himself, or deliberately courted death by presenting himself as an easy target for a sniper's bullet. There were some striking discrepancies in the reports of Edward's death: some described him as being shot by the enemy in full view of his men, others claimed that Edward had insisted on going ahead of the rest of his company, and that his body had only been discovered hours later, after the fighting was over, with a bullet through his head.

These disclosures, I knew from the McMaster letters, had understandably caused Vera Brittain some 'very distressful hours', though she had hastened to reassure Colonel Hudson that she did not believe that her brother would have taken his own life, or gone into battle seeking to be killed. Privately, though, she had increasingly inclined to the opposite point of view, and had dramatized the episode in her novel *Honourable Estate*. What was undeniable was that Edward's final days must have been very bitter. It seemed such a terrible end, to have survived almost the entire war, with the loss of all his closest friends, to have served his country with courage and distinction; and then to have gone to his death in circumstances that must have been unendurable.

After submitting my typescript of *Vera Brittain: A Life* to Chatto in the summer of 1994, I decided to visit Edward's grave at the British military cemetery at Granezza in Northern Italy, 4,000 feet up in the mountains overlooking the Brenta Valley, on the highest corner of the Asiago Plateau. It was a fitting place at which to end my biographical journey. Almost a quarter of a century earlier, Shirley and her then husband, the philosopher Bernard Williams, accompanied by Paul Berry, had scattered Vera Brittain's ashes on her brother's grave. On my trip, Martin Taylor, a friend who worked at the Imperial War Museum in London, joined me. Martin had been extremely helpful in my researches into Vera Brittain's First World War experiences. He was especially interested in the sequence of events that had led to Edward's death as, several years earlier, he had edited and published *Lads*, a highly praised selection of the love poetry of the trenches. It is a moving anthology of the homoerotic verse of the war, revealing the affection between fighting men that often went beyond the bounds of ordinary comradeship. Shortly before we'd set off to Italy, Martin had told me that he was HIV-positive. At night, in the stifling heat of our hotel room in the town of Bassano del Grappa, I watched as he removed his shirt, revealing the horrifying purplish-black lesions on his skin. And I recognized the truth behind Martin's parting remark at the end of his introduction to *Lads*, 'Though we may not have lived through the nightmares of the Western Front, we now have nightmares of our own . . .' Edward Brittain had faced his nightmare, now Martin faced his. Two years later, Martin was dead, at 39.

We found the remains of the trenches, blown out of the rock, in which Edward and his company had spent their last hours before the battle, and then moved on to the grave. Raised sharply above the road, in a small natural amphitheatre, and surrounded by pinewoods climbing towards the skyline, the small cemetery contains the graves of 142 soldiers of the Great War, all of whom were killed during the decisive rout by British and Italian troops of the Austrian army in the summer of 1918.

Few visitors passed this spot. Apart from the cemetery, Granezza, in 1994, consisted of no more than a decaying mountain inn. Only the sound at lunchtimes of local farmers and their families, enjoying their picnics at the gravesides, punctuated the perpetual clanging of cattle bells.

Edward's grave was quickly spotted. A white oblong headstone close to the thick rubble wall bears the simple inscription, 'Captain Edward H. Brittain M.C. Notts & Derby Regiment. 15th June 1918. Aged 22.'

We laid down the flowers we had brought with us, and returned to the road to catch the bus.

Antonia Fraser

Optical Research

Ever since my first nervous steps in the biographical field –
starting to research *Mary, Queen of Scots* 40 years ago – I have been
fascinated by what I have come to term Optical Research. The
term is a good one for tax purposes. Less grandly, one might
describe this activity as going to places and looking at them. But
Optical Research is certainly no tax avoidance scheme: on the
contrary, I have come to believe that my experiences on the geo-
graphical trail have been almost as important in practising the art
of biography, as my hours spent in archives.

With *Mary, Queen of Scots* I visited every conceivable castle,
quagmire, byre or whatever associated with the Queen in three
countries. There was, for example, the trip to Château d'Anet,
home of the legendary beauty Diane de Poitiers, mistress of
Mary's father-in-law, Henri II. I wished to see for myself the
elegant memorial chapel in the black and white colours she made
her own; I wished to admire the architecture of Philibert de
l'Orme who designed it for her with its many crescent moons,
symbol of the goddess Diana, which this sixteenth-century
goddess took as her own symbol. The Château d'Anet was
actually in private hands, but I secured an introduction to the
owner (a South American whom I will call Don Luis). I did so via
Gaston Palewski, an extremely worldly and sophisticated French
Ambassador, who kindly arranged it for me.

On the appointed day, I set forth confidently for Anet, arrived,
was duly received, and asked for a full tour. Don Luis proved to
be both chivalrous and knowledgeable: and as I remember it, he
did not even allow the fact that I had interrupted an enormous

lunch party on the terrace to deter him from showing me every black-and-white nook and cranny which I demanded. A very long time later, Don Luis was interrupted by a servant telling him he was wanted on the telephone. When he came back, he was as courteous as ever. 'So you are Madame Fraser,' he said. 'That was a call from my friend Gaston Palewski arranging for your visit. How happy I am to know your name! And yet a little sad, that you are not just some stranger come out of the blue to visit me, some goddess sent perhaps by the immortal Diana herself . . .' My opinion of South American gallantry and good manners soared even as my rating of French diplomatic efficiency fell.

Less satisfying for me in terms of gallantry was my visit to Stirling Castle. At that time, visitors to the castle were supposed to employ the services of a (paid) guide. However, I was by now under the impression that I knew more about the history of Stirling Castle than any guide; I also wanted to drink in the atmosphere alone, since Stirling, as the traditional nursery of Scottish royal princes, had housed Mary's infant son James. Under the circumstances, I hit upon an expedient which I considered to be brilliant. I decided to pay for a guide, book a solo tour but suggest that my guide did not actually accompany me, instead he should sit out his allocated time in silence.

It did not work out: perhaps it did not deserve to. I duly paid my money, but 'my' guide did not choose to sit out his allotted time in silence. Instead, he took on another complete tour and trailed around just behind me. This enabled him to give his own version of events – well within earshot. Every now and then, however, he indulged in a theatrical pause. Then he would proceed: 'Whisht! But not too loud! There's a very clever young lady here from England and she knows all there is to be known about our poor wee castle. We wouldn't want to disturb the very clever young lady . . .' My feelings of impotent fury may be compared to those of Hilaire Belloc's Lord Canton, who died rather suddenly:

> The insolence of an Italian guide
> Appears to be the reason that he died.

Yet for all the adventures, occasionally ludicrous, which Optical Research produced, I still believe in its value. To take only one example, I would never have understood the pattern of events following the murder of Riccio at Holyrood, had I not been able to go and investigate the layout of the palace myself. It was the tiny cramped size of Mary's room where the crime took place which explained to me more vividly than any document how the events of that tragic occasion must have fallen out; just as the correspondingly enormous size of the fireplace – virtually half one wall – showed me that the dashing-out of all the candles would still have left a very well-lit room.

Much later I had somewhat the same experience – understanding the situation properly for the first time – when visiting the hidey-holes constructed for the forbidden Catholic priests. You can't really understand the appallingly cramped conditions of a hidey-hole in which the forbidden Catholic priests were hidden unless you try to cram yourself in – and when I was working on both *Charles II* and *The Gunpowder Plot* I did cram myself in, and reflect: 'I'm here for five minutes and I've just had tea and I'm going to have dinner. What about Father Garnet the Jesuit who spent ten days here with a biscuit and a pot of quince jam?' (Which is what his hostess happened to have in her hand when the dreaded cry went up: 'The searchers are coming.') 'Or what about Charles II, I'm 5′ 8″, but he was 6′ 3″. And they were in danger of their lives if they came out.'

With Cromwell, it was a trip of enormous significance for me when I went in his footsteps to Ireland. I came freshly from Huntingdon where Cromwell was born and where he was also MP, and of course all round there the local hero. Now I was in Ireland, so on getting out of my car at Drogheda, I assumed everyone was going to be equally helpful. What a mistake! Seeing two priests and a nun I said: 'Can you direct me to St Mary's church, and where was Cromwell's mound, please?' At the mention of the word Cromwell, all I can say is that they looked at me with horror (because Cromwell massacred the Irish Catholics), jumped into their car, and without answering, started to wind up the windows. At this my companion said: 'You really are an idiot. This is Ireland, remember, where Cromwell killed the Catholics. Let me deal with it.' And he went up to the nun (who crossed herself) and said in a very oily voice: 'This is the daughter of the holy Catholic Lord Longford, who for some extraordinary reason known entirely to herself, is writing a biography of the wicked and tyrannous usurper Oliver Cromwell, could you tell me where the church is . . .' And the mention of my father's Catholic name satisfied this Irish nun, so we found it. 'That-a-way,' she said. In one swoop I had learned something about the continuing reputation of Cromwell in Ireland which reading acres of books wouldn't have told me.

With *The Six Wives of Henry VIII* it's the tombs or graves of the six Queens which are significant. So much do their respective tombs symbolize their fates, that I am thinking – not altogether frivolously – of organizing a day's pilgrimage to all six, which you could quite easily do. Let us begin with the disgraced Queens first: the two who were executed within the Tower of London, Anne Boleyn and Katherine Howard. The decapitated bodies were buried obscurely in the adjacent chapel, and even when Elizabeth came to the throne, it is significant that she made no attempt to rescue the body of her mother and give it decent burial. It was not until the late nineteenth century, inspired by Queen Victoria, that their bodies were rescued and, with those of other decapitated state prisoners, buried decently beneath plaques beneath the altar.

Jane Seymour of course had to be buried where the King could join her because she was the mother of his son. So she is buried beneath the choir pavement in St George's Chapel. I feel her slight coffin must have been crushed by the huge coffin of the King buried literally on top of her ten years later. So no one ever thinks of her, only of him. Anna of Cleves has an equally typically obscure burial: in fact it's right on the main altar of Westminster Abbey, on the right as you look at it. A verger told me that at the last coronation, a special balcony was built over her tomb in which the Queen Mother and Prince Charles – then a little boy – sat. So there she is, so close to the centre of events, and completely obscured.

Catherine Parr is buried at Sudeley in Gloucestershire. In the nineteenth century she was sort of tidied up and given a huge marble Victorian tomb by Sir Gilbert Scott, making of her the submissive Victorian wife. Which she wasn't – but everyone always thought she was. Catherine of Aragon on the other hand, who was buried in Peterborough Cathedral, is triumphant at last, because her burial place has become a real place of pilgrimage, with banners to mark the spot, and there are always flowers there. One of the banners was put up by all the Katherines in the country, the other by Queen Mary. It seems to me that that is symbolic of her defeat in life, her victory in death.

The most gratifying result of this attention to Optical Research has been the number of readers who write to me saying: 'You know, we used your book as a guide on a recent visit to . . .' although I have to say that a fair proportion of them go on to complain about the weight of my books.

Frances Spalding

Catching Trout

I didn't choose to write biography: it crept up on me, almost by chance, and became a way of life. And, like other professions, it encourages certain ploys. Even when I'm not researching a person's life, I sometimes hear myself chatting to strangers – on stalled trains or in empty pubs – in a give-away manner: asking the open-ended question; pursuing small details; currying trust through a mixture of sympathy and restraint; and, sometimes, successfully targeting an interest that releases a hidden passion and opens a window on to another's life.

Talking with the dead is still better: they are there when you need them; conversations can be picked up exactly where you left off; and they never pay any attention to your clothes, so self-presentation is not a problem. The conversation, of course, as you read and interrogate a person's letters and diaries, goes on inside your head. In time, an extraordinary intimacy develops which, while the book is in progress, remains almost completely hidden. Even your spouse or partner is unlikely to be aware of the extent of your infidelity, of the obsessive amount of thought, the heedless energy, time and money you have spent in order to be alone with your subject. It's almost irrational. But perhaps biography, to be truly humane, needs to be a little irrational.

How, then, did I come to be attracted to this labour-intensive, maverick genre? At the start, my intentions were respectable, even career-orientated. I wanted to write a doctoral thesis on the man who woke England to modern art. This was Roger Fry, whose simple directive – to look at form – cut through barriers of class and education and removed the boundaries separating the present from the past and one culture from another. 'Once you'd read Roger Fry, the whole thing was there,' said Henry Moore who as a student had found his *Vision and Design* in Leeds Art Reference Library. Fry's name crops up in numerous memoirs and biographies. But, in the 1970s, art historians and critics treated him dismissively, making reference to only a handful of his extensive writings and throwing in derogatory comments about his paintings. The only book available on Fry when I began my research was Virginia Woolf's biography. This skips lightly and perceptively over his life and offers an impressionistic study of his achievement. It left me wanting to know more.

So, in chase after something which I did not then know would end in biography, I embarked on extensive reading and went to see Roger Fry's daughter, Pamela Diamand. As a postgraduate student, I needed to obtain her good will, to ask for access to documents still in her possession and for help with the names and addresses of those in possession of her father's paintings. I remember struggling with the wooden gate in the rickety fence that fronted her large house in Clarendon Road, Holland Park, an area of London with which I was then unfamiliar. Nowadays when I revisit the area and walk down that street, I find myself saying, this is where it all began, that journey into life and other lives. This is where my fascination with the past took hold.

I made many visits to 48 Clarendon Road. The walls of the house were thickly hung with pictures. Mementoes of all kinds littered the mantelpieces and emerged from tallboys and chests of drawers. On one occasion, when we were discussing the size of Victorian families, Pamela pulled out of a drawer her grand-mother's nineteenth-century black Quaker dress, and showed me how it could be adjusted as pregnancy progressed.

One afternoon I was handed a bundle of letters written by the young Roger Fry to his mother. As I untied the pink tape a card fell out. It contained a short list indicating, mostly by means of a single word, the contents of these letters. Written in purple ink, its elegant but spiky hand was instantly recognizable as Virginia Woolf's. It added another fragment to these precious shards from the past, and I found it strangely moving. I must also admit that the casual nature of Woolf's list-making had a breezy appeal.

There were less happy discoveries. Nowadays, I am aware that obstacles are par for the course, but then I was devastated to learn that the bulk of Roger Fry's papers had gone on long-term loan to a scholar who had vanished. Eventually, this problem was solved and the Fry Papers joined the archives in King's College, Cambridge. I lodged in vacation periods in student rooms, spent six hours a day in King's College Library reading, note-taking or transcribing documents, seated beneath the fierce gloom emitted by a bust of Napoleon. Outside one window a magnolia grandiflora bloomed. On summer evenings swifts dipped low over the sweep of grass in front of St John's. Roger Fry, while at Cambridge, wrote to his mother: 'Life does not seem to flow with the same dull round of increasing common-place within a quarter of a mile of King's bridge from where one can now watch the golden chestnut and lime leaves flutter down through the rising purple haze on to the river.' I knew what he meant. Nor was my enchantment with the past dimmed when, in King's dining-hall, an elderly don asked: 'Who are you, my dear, and what are you working on?' I explained that I was studying Roger Fry's extensive manuscripts and correspondence. He threw back his head and laughed. 'Oh,' he said, 'that old trout!' The librarian Dr A. N. L. Munby had a similar reaction. On learning of my existence, he appeared round the corner of a stack one day and remarked, in a puzzled tone: 'It's very odd – people like you turning up and writing about those who once were my friends.'

I was still working towards, not a biography, but a thesis which was going to connect the twists and turns in Fry's critical thought with his development as a painter. To this end I needed to track down as many of his paintings as I could. There was a good selection in public museums and galleries up and down the country, but many remained in the possession of his family and his friends or their descendants. Often I found myself looking at his paintings while listening to anecdotes about his behaviour, interests and idiosyncrasies. As he grew in my mind, I began to realize that his extraordinary energy spilled into many fields and that he resisted compartmentalization. My dissertation began to expand into something more generous, if less academically creditable.

On one occasion I found myself seated in a house in Keat's Grove, Hampstead. With its owner, Marjorie Rackstraw, who had been a friend of one of Fry's sisters, I had gone round various rooms looking at her Roger Fry paintings. We were now having a genteel tea in a room furnished with a spare elegance that matched the distinction which hung about Marjorie Rackstraw's tall, thin, frail frame. My questions were almost certainly clumsy and inept. I cannot remember what it was that brought the following reply. 'During . . . the war,' she said slowly, 'I worked . . . for the Quaker War Victims' Relief Fund . . . in the district of the Marne and the Meuse.' In my childhood, when adults referred to 'the war', the Second World War was what everyone had in mind. To find myself in the mid-1970s talking with someone whose memories and experience took us back to the 1914–18 war, its razed villages and devastated landscape, was for me, in that gentle environment with the summer light glancing off the furniture, oddly disturbing. I was made aware of a ribbon of time, running between the past and present, which my question had caused to vibrate.

I had discovered that the past is not just past, not merely something out there which one can study: it is also an active ingredient which can inhabit, thicken and challenge the present. This realization coincided with a bit of luck. As I was finishing my dissertation, a letter arrived. It was from a publisher who wanted a book on Roger Fry that dealt with his life and work. The result was my first stab at biography.

But it is my next book which I regard as my first proper biography. Fry had led me to Vanessa Bell. Reading their correspondence, I had become intrigued by this woman, then the most silent and least known figure within Bloomsbury. I began contemplating a book on her and went back to King's College to read more of her papers. There I learnt that her son, Professor Quentin Bell, had been approached by two Americans, both of whom wanted to write Vanessa Bell's life. That evening I walked round the dark streets in a state of almost complete despair. Eventually I went to a public telephone box in the Market Place (there were no mobile phones then and no telephone in my lodgings). I rang Quentin, and then, at his insistence, his sister Angelica Garnett. Both agreed that I could join the competition for the right to do a biography of Vanessa Bell. We all had to produce one chapter and a synopsis. I did so and won the opportunity to write what was, for me, a deeply moving and hugely enjoyable book which, I'm proud to say, is still in print today. But I will never forget those agonized phone calls and the heavy crash as each additional coin descended the box, loudly punctuating my attempts to sound calm, rational and intelligent, amid the stink and grime of a public telephone box.

Since then I have written biographies of the poet Stevie Smith, the artists John Minton and Duncan Grant, and of the woodengraver and author of *Period Piece*, Gwen Raverat. I walk around now with my head stuffed full of memories, my own and other people's, with the past and present inextricably meshed. I cannot explain why tiny, seemingly inconsequential facts become ineradicable. Whenever I pass Marchmont Street in Bloomsbury, for instance, I recollect that here Vanessa Bell had her last sighting of her friend Janie Bussy ('quite changed, stouter and looking more decidedly French'), who tragically died soon after, owing to a faulty old-fashioned gas water-heater in the bathroom at 51 Gordon Square. Recently, when making a radio programme on Stevie Smith with Jackie Kay, which involved a return to Palmers Green, I stood outside Stevie Smith's very ordinary red-brick terraced house in Avondale Road and watched two boys playing inside an upstairs room. Was it still, I wondered, 'A house expecting strength as it is strong/A house of aristocratic mould that looks apart/When tears fall; counts despair/Derisory . . ./. . . at heart/A house of mercy'? And when I have to 'appear' at an event, I nowadays hear Vanessa Bell's despairing admonition that neatness – she frequently resorted to safety pins – is the thing to strive for in middle age.

Amid the pleasures of writing biography, there have been many disappointments, failures and rejections. But now and then you hit it right. I happen to be writing this piece in Sheffield and this morning the old man next door called out to me.

'Frances, can you write?'

'Sort of.'

'Come here, then.'

I went, knowing that the issue was his difficulty in obtaining a rebate on his council tax which has risen beyond his means. We both struggled with the spelling of osteomyelitis, but I wrote the necessary letter to the Benefits Officer, answering her questions in, I think, a satisfactory manner. I hope it will do the trick.

Andrew Roberts

La-Di-Da

One's first book always occupies a special place in one's heart. Memories flood back, old, half-forgotten associations are renewed, nostalgia – which at the age of 40 I now recognize as a powerful force in my psychological make-up – is given full rein.

My first book was entitled *The Holy Fox*, and subtitled *A Biography of Lord Halifax*; it was published in 1991. Now, as I look down the acknowledgements list of the 100 or so people whom I interviewed for that book, I find the names of only three people that knew Lord Halifax who are still alive today. (I shan't mention them by name, since I would not want to excite any untoward intimations of mortality in them.) Since it drew pretty heavily on personal recollections, it is a book that simply could not be written today.

The interviewing of witnesses to great historical events is a delicate process, one for which I was ill-prepared when I embarked on my project in 1987. Although they virtually never consciously attempt to mislead – indeed they are usually tremendously keen to help historians try to get the record straight – there are huge pitfalls to relying on them for accurate memories of the events of even a decade ago, let alone half a century. As stories are told and re-told over time they tend to acquire the barnacles of exaggeration that tend to adhere to an oft-sailed story. Once contemporaries have started to die, thus removing anyone capable of gainsaying the story from personal knowledge, the tales often tend further to grow taller in the telling.

This does not ever make them not worth listening to. Many of the most fascinating and stimulating times of my life have been spent hearing the reminiscences of the diplomats and soldiers, politicians and writers of the post-Great War, Appeasement and Second World War eras. I deem myself incredibly fortunate to have been able to spend four years visiting so many of the political figures of the interwar years to hear their recollections of the personalities and politics of the period from 1920 to 1945.

Yet their recollections tend to require strenuous double-checking against published and unpublished sources before they can ever be allowed between hard covers as serious, objective history. As a depressing but in my experience an accurate general rule, the heartier one's laugh at the end of the anecdote, the less likely the story is to have been true. On occasion it seemed almost cruel for me to mention evidence that proved that a much-loved story simply could not have been true – because the diplomat was in another country at the time, say, or because the chronology of the tale suffered from dire internal contradictions. On those occasions I would always laugh at the punch-line, but then merely refrain from including the tale in the book. No one ever complained that his or her story never appeared.

If even Sir Winston Churchill, writing in 1948, could get wrong the date and time of the crucial May 1940 meeting in the Cabinet room at Number 10 that made him Prime Minister, as well as mistaking the number of people present – there were four, not three – then it is small wonder that many factual inaccuracies have crept into so many lesser stories, that are, after all, often told as much for the sake of entertainment as an attempt at objective history.

When a story is just too good to leave out of a book there are a number of ways that a biographer can gently warn his reader of its apocryphal nature. 'Friends claim that . . .', 'It is said that . . .' or 'The story goes that . . .' are all pretty blatant signposts to the reader that the author no longer regards himself as being on oath.

While I was researching *The Holy Fox* there were many stories that I regarded as amusing, interesting – intriguing even – but ultimately as unreliable evidence. Some were probably worth following up, others were doubtless entirely true, but none were so easily verifiable that I could honestly stand by their veracity. There is – or at least there should be – a kind of Hippocratic Oath for historians, a line that should not be crossed between actuality and speculation. I never think much of those historians you occasionally read who claim to know exactly what their subjects were thinking at any particular time, without the express use of a diary or correspondence to prove it.

Jasper Rootham, who was Neville Chamberlain's assistant private secretary between September 1938 and October 1939, told me that 'One of the most distasteful things I had to do when I was on duty alone at Number 10, close to when the war broke out, [was to] open a communication for the attention of the Prime Minister from MI5. It was the transcript of a conversation between Churchill and [the Russian Ambassador] Ivan Maisky to do with the Anglo-Russian talks . . . MI5 were tapping the Russians; I'm assuming they weren't tapping Winston.' Yet from further remarks he then made off-the-record, it was clear that Rootham in fact believed that MI5 was indeed spying on Winston Churchill for the Chamberlain Government. Given the attitude towards Churchill by the Establishment at that time, I think it entirely possible that Churchill's phone was bugged by the security services, although we will not know for sure until about the end of the twenty-first century.

On a lighter note, the ninth and last Duke of Portland, who had served in the Foreign Office from 1915 and who had attended the Lausanne Conference of 1922 before becoming the wartime chairman of the Joint Intelligence Committee, had his own theory about the true cause for the outbreak of the Second World War.

Speaking of the conference, he recalled: 'The French were being very tiresome because we weren't backing them in their desire to occupy the Ruhr. In Paris on New Year's Eve, Curzon was to join Bonar Law to bully Poincaré – not easy, but still . . . They got to Paris and Curzon went to stay at the Ritz. The Marquis had difficulty in sleeping as a Roumanian couple [were fornicating in] the room next to his and the walls were rather thin and they kept Curzon awake. The next day Curzon was tired, Bonar Law was very weak and Poincaré got his way and they went into the Ruhr, which was the foundation of Hitler. All because of the fornication of this Roumanian couple!'

Portland's was what Marxist historiographers would call a monocausal, non-determinist explanation of history, and it sadly couldn't find a place in my book. (In those days, I cared deeply what reviewers said of my work; if I was writing it today it might have been a different story.)

Lord Curzon's daughter, Lady Alexandra Metcalfe, was a fountain of stories and high-quality gossip, not least because of her and Lord Halifax's entirely platonic adoration of each other. I returned to her flat in Eaton Place again and again, and as long as I stayed off studiously delineated topics – her love affairs with Sir Oswald Mosley and the Italian ambassador Count Dino Grandi, for example – she was very happy to reminisce. She enjoyed recalling taking tea with Goebbels, hearing Chaim Weizmann telling her in the Dorchester during the Blitz how Britain should be manufacturing petrol from dead leaves, staying with Churchill at Ditchley Park when they heard that Rudolf Hess had landed in Scotland, and quoting Lady Diana Cooper saying of Duff: 'I don't mind who he's in love with, but I do mind whether he's got a cold.'

She was entirely *compos mentis*, but would occasionally say things such as, 'It's terrible to have people sucked out of aeroplanes', apropos of nothing in particular, which tended to leave me in fits of giggles. 'I had a smashing eightieth birthday dinner given me by the Cambodian Communists,' she told me of her time as chairwoman of the Save the Children Fund, 'they showed me the 8,000 skulls of people killed by Pol Pot.' For this treat she had turned down the offer of a birthday dinner at the Ritz that was to be attended by the Queen Mother. The twinkle of malice was never too far from those flashing blue eyes of hers, especially when it came to her lifelong *bête noire*: 'Diana Mosley is always talking about the Windsors nowadays,' she once told me. 'Why, I'll never know. She only knew them *very* late in life.'

Valentine Lawford was Halifax's private secretary and the last of the dandies. I was invited to have a drink with him in the library at Brooks's one evening in August 1989, before his dinner guests arrived. From his impeccable manners, his charm, wit and beautifully cut Prince of Wales-check suit, I caught the faintest scented whiff of that aesthetic wartime London peopled by the likes of Harold Nicolson, James Lees-Milne and James Pope-Hennessy. He lived at the almost aesthetically onomato-poeic address of Tiffany Road, Oyster Bay, Long Island, and as I came upon him he was dedicating to the Duchess of Buccleuch a copy of a book of photographs taken by his close friend Horst P. Horst.

Lawford stayed with Chips Channon at Belgrave Square during the Blitz, when Channon was PPS to Rab Butler, Halifax's Under-Secretary at the Foreign Office. He was therefore a doubly excellent source. He freely admitted that he had become, as he put it in a way that for some reason didn't sound affected, 'a *diploamatist*', primarily for aesthetic and social reasons and 'because unlike my family I could never be a farmer or a soldier'. (That much was clear from a glance at his light-blue polka-dotted bow-tie.)

As with so many of the diplomats I interviewed, his air of ironic detachment collapsed at the mention of the names of the Cambridge spies who had not only betrayed their country and the Foreign Office, they all felt, but also their friends, their colleges, their schools, their class, and, in the expressed views of many of my interlocutors, their own souls.

'Blunt was a revolting deceiver with a *la-di-da* air,' recalled Lawford. 'He was older than me at Cambridge; he looked like a camel. I associated him with Burgess years before he was unmasked. I'd thrown a banana at them as they came out of Trinity Great Court together.' Once again I didn't feel this information, though amusing, was necessarily worthy of inclusion in the book. The unmasking of traitors depended on something more substantial than the hurling of fruit 30 years earlier, and although the incident begged any number of questions, Lawford had already moved on to Burgess: 'Guy was just dirty, very grubby and sweaty. I can't imagine how anybody could have made him out to be a Don Juan.' Lawford seemed genuinely embarrassed that, as he recalled, 'Kim Philby's grandmother's brother married my mother's sister's stepdaughter.'

Easily the most shocking thing that I was told came from Sir Denis Rickett, the All Souls fellow between 1929 and 1949 who was closely involved in the Manhattan Project, the Tube Alloys operation and the whole genesis of the nuclear bomb. As personal assistant to the Lord President of the Council in 1945, he briefed the incoming Prime Minister Clement Attlee on atomic issues immediately after the general election, and prior to the attacks on Hiroshima and Nagasaki.

I had long wondered why it had been necessary to drop two bombs, since the effects of the first one were undeniable even to Japanese fanaticism, and I asked whether a demonstration of the destructive capacity of nuclear fission to Japanese scientists in the

Mongolian desert, say, might not have had the same result? Rickett's explanation to me back in November 1988 I still find rather chilling: 'It was a political necessity to drop the bombs on Japan after they'd spent six billion dollars on it,' he told me. 'They had to drop two to test them. One was plutonium and the other uranium. You had to test both.' It was not a decision that Lord Halifax had been involved in, so this too escaped publication, but the idea of upwards of 118,000 Japanese civilians perishing in order to justify public expenditure and to 'test' the different effects of the two types of weaponry is one that at least gives pause for thought.

Another rather perturbing witness was Reinhard Spitzy, an engaging and talkative person who looked uncannily like Walter Matthau, with drooping jowls and a large red nose. He had joined the Nazi Party in 1931 and had been involved in the attempted putsch against Dollfuss in Vienna in 1934. Three years later he became Ribbentrop's private secretary, in which capacity he attended the Munich Conference. In his autobiography, slightly disconcertingly entitled *How We Squandered the Reich*, there are photographs of Spitzy standing in between Hitler and Chamberlain, almost edging Mussolini out of the picture. 'Nobody is a monster from the egg,' he told me. 'Hitler was no monster. He became a monster in 1942. I would have become one too in his circumstances.' I could well believe it, especially after Spitzy told me that he had had to live in an Argentinian swamp for ten years after managing to escape from Germany in 1945.

Back in September 1989 when I interviewed him in his Kensington hotel, Spitzy's remarks such as 'Czechoslovakia was a ridiculous state. The word is ridiculous . . . an invention of Clemenceau' just sounded like unreconstructed Nazism. Today, Czechoslovakia is indeed no more. Similarly, the way that he looked forward to the Anschluss of East and West Germany – 'We have got the same right as Slavs to form blocs. We could reunite. That damned idiot [Woodrow] Wilson cheated us' – made me uneasy, especially when only two months after our interview the Berlin Wall was suddenly pulled down. Today the experiment has been shown to have worked; back then I found it all distinctly unsettling.

The nonagenarian John Codrington I interviewed over lunch at the Beefsteak Club, where he was one of the oldest and best-loved members. David Irving, who once had a reputation as an historian (at least in 1989), had written a book about how British Intelligence had murdered the Polish leader General Sikorski, who had died when his plane crashed while taking off from Gibraltar in 1943. 'Hang on a minute,' expostulated John, 'I was SIS station chief in Gib in 1943. If Churchill had ordered anyone to kill him, it would have been me. And I distinctly remember never having been asked.'

An even older interviewee was Count Edward Raczynski, who was 96 when I saw him in his flat in Lennox Gardens in October 1988 for the first of three fascinating meetings. The Polish ambassador from 1934 to 1945, he became Poland's foreign minister from 1943 and later her president-in-exile. Completely blind, wearing a three-piece tweed suit and surrounded by paintings of his family's various palaces in Poland that had long since been confiscated by the communists, Raczynski was charm personified. He had known Padarewski, Pilsudski, Sikorski and Colonel Beck, and his memory was as sharp as the creases on his well-pressed trousers. He had also known Molotov and Litvinov, Churchill and Eden, Benes and Jan Masaryk, Edward VIII and Ribbentropp, and so was a superb source for my book. Raczynski's recollections of Ribbentropp – 'a self-made cheeky fellow who saluted with his jackboots' – were funny, especially when he discussed Ribbentropp's wife's German champagne business in a tone which made it quite clear that he did not believe that true champagne could ever be produced outside France.

There was a world of sadness in his memories of what the twentieth century had wrought on his homeland, a place he had been banned from visiting since 1945. Yet he spoke about such horrors as the crushing by the Nazis, within binocular view of the Red Army, of the Warsaw Uprising, without bitterness but simply in heart-wrenching terms of the terrible wrong that had again and again been done his people. He told me he did not want to be buried in Poland until it was free.

Raczynski was keen to dispel the myth that Polish *uhlans* ever attacked German tanks with their lances in 1939. 'The Polish Army was very well trained, they were not like natives!' he said. 'The idea that we attacked tanks out of passion and courage, that was legend.' A man of great passion and courage himself, Raczynski lived to see his country liberated from communism. President Lech Walesa, whom he greatly admired, flew to London to attend his hundredth birthday party, and today he is buried in a free Poland, according to his original wishes.

Other memories that have come back to me as I looked through my interview file for *The Holy Fox* include David Astor recalling his pre-war friendship with Adam von Trott and his mother's asking Stalin 'how long he'd go on ruling by Tsarist methods?'; of Isaiah Berlin saying that the most malicious game an Englishman could play was to speculate who would have collaborated if the Germans had invaded, before going on to play exactly that game himself; of Rab Butler's widow denouncing Harold Macmillan as 'a downright liar'; of the nonagenarian Indian writer Nirad Chaudhuri telling me he had no fear of death but an absolute terror of a factual error creeping into his *Times* obituary, and of the wonderful Lord Colyton, a gentleman to the end of his elegant fingertips, recalling the words of the

Colonial Office porter in June 1940 when he'd heard the news of France's capitulation, and told his colleague: 'Good news, Bill, we're in the final!'

Halifax's niece, the Hon. Mrs Julian Chetwynd, was born in September 1899, and when I visited her in Cadogan Square she recalled the parties to celebrate the official opening of Lutyens' New Delhi when her uncle was viceroy; Lady Elliot of Harwood told me that her father Sir Charles Tennant had been born in 1823 (to hear someone refer to Herbert Asquith as 'my brother-in-law' sounded somewhat surreal even in 1990); when Douglas Fairbanks Jr walked through Claridge's to tell me about attending deb parties in the 1920s with Halifax's daughter Anne, his fine bearing, pencil moustache and carnation in buttonhole turned female heads even though he was well into his 80s.

In the course of four years' research I found nothing but charm, assistance and generosity from that heroic generation. They might have been elegant, and occasionally effete, but they also faced down and saw off a tyranny far worse than any that I hope our time will ever have to encounter. That does not mean, however, that all their memories can be used in what must attempt to be, for better or worse, an objective work of history.

Originally delivered as a lecture in 2003 to the AGM of the Friends of National Libraries.

Ian Thomson

My Race Not to Be the Second Primo

When I arrived in Italy in early 1991 to begin my biography of Primo Levi, I could not have imagined that it would take ten years to complete. Progress was hampered by the arrival of my three children; the buggy in the hall was always a reminder of other duties. I was the first biographer to work on Levi's life, yet I was almost beaten to the bookshops by a rival. Perhaps I should not have been surprised: biography was always a competitive business. When Dr Johnson died in 1784, Boswell had spent 20 years gathering material for his *Life*. He set to work immediately, but his rival Hester Thrale pipped him to the bookstalls with her *Anecdotes of the Late Samuel Johnson*. Biographies on the same subject often tend to pile up at anniversaries. The tercentenary of Purcell's death in 1995 saw no fewer than four books published on the composer, and when Bob Dylan finally turned 60 in 2001, a slew of biographies crashed the party. In Primo Levi's case, however, sheer bad luck dictated that two books should appear on him at the same time.

Months before his suicide in 1987, Primo Levi had appointed an Italian critic as his official biographer. Nothing came of the book, and after Levi's death his widow understandably wanted no business with biographers. I was lucky to have interviewed Levi shortly before he died, and subsequently had access to his sister for vital information. Indeed, by the time my rival came to Italy, I had already spoken to most of Levi's surviving friends and relatives. Consequently I passed her only once – when an interviewee booked us in at the same time. I had gone back to check some facts with him when my competitor unexpectedly emerged from the lavatory. It was like a scene in a bad Woody Allen film (or perhaps a Henry James short story). 'Are you the famous Carole Angier?' I asked, and she held out her hand. 'Are you the famous Ian Thomson?'

Writing and researching a biography with a rival at one's back can be a nightmare. It is impossible to forget that whatever you write will eventually be judged against the other. For me, the rivalry created terrific pressures. Vexed by Carole Angier's presence, I invented foolish nicknames for her: 'C&A' (after the high street shop which went out of business) or, less often, 'Look Back in Angier'. Years later I learned that my rival had done the same to me: I was 'It' to her, from my own initials. Clearly I had been a thorn in Angier's side. 'It's been odd following in your foot-steps,' she subsequently told me. Indeed, virtually everyone she approached for an interview had already spoken to me. My rival even became convinced that I was sending her Voodoo* coffin nails in the post (though she later confessed in the London *Guardian* that the nails had in fact been cheap plastic hairbrush teeth).

One may laugh; at the time the competition was hell. There were a number of false but disturbing alarms in the build-up to publication. My biography had been announced in the pub-lisher's catalogue years before it was finished, and I often received misleading intelligence that my rival was on the verge of com-pletion. To ensure that our biographies came out simultaneously (rather than mine lagging fatally behind), I had to correct page proofs at frantic speed. Manuscript bundles would be delivered to

---

*On the subject of Voodoo and biography, Graham Greene reportedly put a spell on his long-enduring biographer Norman Sherry. Over dry martinis, Greene told him: 'Norman, I shall be alive for Volume 1 of your biography, but I shall die before Volume 2. And you, my dear Norman, will not live to see completion of Volume 3.' Greene was right about Volumes 1 and 2, but not, fortunately, about Volume 3.

my house by Random House motorbike couriers. The pressure was awful, though my young son at least thrilled to the sight of the bikers in their leathers (as did my wife, I'm afraid).

In the interests of concision and, I hoped, readability, at the eleventh hour I cut 120,000 words from my typescript. Finally, a woman rushed up to me at the printer's, cradling a finished copy: 'It's a boy!' she announced. However, I found it hard to smile: for a decade that wretched biography had hung round my neck like an albatross, and I had come to loathe both it and biography. As I expected, the books were reviewed together in all the national newspapers. Competition was fierce, but for one improbable week (according to the *Evening Standard*) one of the two Levi lives was the London bestseller after Alan Titchmarsh's *How to Be a Gardener* and Margaret Thatcher's *Statecraft*.

I pitied the reviewers. They had to wade through a combined total of 1,500 pages and it must have been hard for them to give a balanced assessment of both works. (Anthony Julius, former lawyer to Diana, Princess of Wales, was so overwhelmed by the task in *The Times* that he mis-spelt my name not just once, but an impressive total of 15 times.) Luckily, my rival and I had strikingly different approaches to biography, and this made it easier for the book-buyer to decide which one they liked. I doubt I shall ever read my competitor's book (life is too short); nevertheless, I understand that mine is 300 pages shorter than hers, and reportedly much cooler in its appraisals. Moreover, although I had met Levi and she had not, I refused to put myself on first-name terms with him. My intention had been to write a measured work that I hoped might inspire trust in the reader. My competitor's instinct, on the contrary, had apparently been to make a drama of her own research and empathize imaginatively with 'Primo'. (This sort of biography is increasingly common, I suppose, in our touchy-feely, Blairite times.)

Incredible as it may seem, rival biographers may benefit from each other. Angier was a spur for me to excel and in my diligence I believe I rooted out more people who had known Levi, and located more documentation than I might otherwise have done. In fact much of the material I unearthed had not been seen before, and to my knowledge others have not yet picked up on Albert Speer's extraordinary letters about Primo Levi. (On New Year's Day 1976, the repentant former Nazi had written to Primo Levi's German friend, Hety Schmitt-Maas, that he had 'skimmed' Levi's great prison memoir, *If This Is a Man*; on hearing this extraordinary news, Levi wrote – in English – to Hety: 'It looks to me like an odd dream that this book of mine, born in the mud of Auschwitz, is going to sail upstream – to one of the very Almighties of that time!' Unfortunately, no correspondence has yet come to light between Levi and Speer.)

Once our biographies had been launched, we were locked into an undignified struggle for publicity. Bravely, we agreed to appear together on television. In the BBC make-up room I was astonished to encounter Mickey Dolenz from the 1960s Monkees pop group, who was then touring Britain. As I emerged to confront my rival under the glare of the studio lights, a Monkees smash-hit ran through my mind. '*Then I saw her face – I'm a believer, I couldn't leave her if I tried.*' (Which was certainly distracting.) At the Edinburgh Book Festival we met again for a head-to-head debate. In the 'hospitality tent' (a ghastly reproduction of a Mongolian yurt complete with scatter cushions), we greeted each other warily. Afterwards we were made to sit side by side at the table and flog our biographies like fishwives. Some wag had prominently displayed piles of them next to the journalist James Naughtie's book about Tony Blair and Gordon Brown, *The Rivals*.

To my relief, while some critics (several of whom, admittedly, were Angier's friends) liked the rival biography, others preferred mine. However, in the war of two biographies, only one will ultimately survive: let the public decide which one that should be. In the meantime, I have been touched to see our books billed on the Amazon website as 'Perfect Partners' ('Buy Both and Save £10!'). We have been wedded in cyberspace, my dear 'C&A', if nowhere else.

Lucasta Miller

Stuff with Raw Edges

I have a secret fear that I might never again be allowed to see any of the manuscripts in the Pierpont Morgan collection in New York. I hope the librarian wasn't looking, but when I called up a section of Charlotte Brontë's 'Roe Head Journal' – the fragmentary diary she kept while a young teacher at the Miss Woolers' school at Roe Head – I found my eyes filling with inconvenient tears. To my horror, one nearly made it onto the priceless document.

What made the experience so unexpectedly moving – and I'd been in a cynical bad mood that day – was the sense that I was intruding into a private space. This scrap of paper, covered in tiny writing, recorded the minute-by-minute secret fantasies of a woman who had been dead for nearly a century and a half. I was overwhelmed by an almost necromantic sense of the past coming to life, and could understand for the first time the emotional lure of relics. Rationalist though I am, the fact that Charlotte Brontë and I had both touched that piece of paper – which was never intended for anyone's eyes but her own – gave me a thrill that I'm almost too embarrassed to record.

I had a very different experience in the British Library with some other Charlotte Brontë manuscripts, letters this time. When I called them up I found myself faced not with a sheaf of naked papers but with a forbiddingly heavy wooden brass-hinged box. Inside were a number of framed glass sheets, vaguely resembling the sort of photographic plates one imagines Julia Margaret Cameron might have used. Each document was sandwiched between glass, visible to the reader yet literally untouchable.

Once I looked at the four letters, it soon became apparent why they might need to be protected in this way. Cutting across some of them are a series of jagged, wound-like tears, which make them frailer than they might otherwise be for their 150-odd years. They clearly betray the fact that they were once ripped up, but also, more extraordinarily, that the pieces were subsequently reassembled like jigsaw puzzles and surgically stitched together with thread.

Now famously referred to as the 'Heger letters', the documents' original recipient was Constantin Heger, the Belgian professor who taught Brontë while she was studying in Brussels in the early 1840s, and with whom she fell in love. As material objects, they seem to embody the tense, triangular relationship between the woman who wrote them, the man who tore them up, and the woman – Heger's wife – who pieced them back together.

These letters were clearly not meant to survive, let alone be encased in a literary reliquary to be admired and scrutinized by future generations. Yet had they stayed in the wastepaper basket where Constantin Heger tossed them, and been thrown out with the rest of the rubbish, our view of Charlotte Brontë would be very different from what it is today. The violent emotions she expressed to Heger, in French, give a biographical grounding to the passion in her novels, particularly *Villette*, in which the heroine's tutor and lover Paul Emanuel is clearly based on the real-life professor. Had the letters disappeared, Brontë's literary treatment of romantic love might have seemed as mysteriously impersonal as that of her enigmatic sister Emily in *Wuthering Heights*.

The sensitive nature of the letters' contents was immediately apparent to Charlotte Brontë's friend and first biographer, Elizabeth Gaskell, who came across them on a fact-finding trip to Brussels in 1856. Keen to discover more about her subject's time as a student and English teacher at the Pensionnat Heger, Gaskell arrived at the school to find, to her embarrassment, that Madame refused to see her. The reason for this rudeness soon became apparent when Monsieur, who did receive her, showed or read her what Brontë had written to him a decade earlier.

The discovery of a secret unrequited passion must have had a powerful effect on the biographer. After first reading *Villette* in 1853, Gaskell had guessed that Lucy Snowe's love for Paul Emanuel had some autobiographical basis, telling a friend that 'it reveals depths in [Brontë's] mind, aye, and in her *heart* too which I doubt if ever any one has fathomed'. The letters may have made Charlotte instantly more fathomable, but what Gaskell had never suspected was that the object of her subject's feelings had been a married man.

As a novelist with a tendency to melodrama, Gaskell might naturally have received the revelation as a gift. In her quest for a good narrative, she had often been tempted to embellish workaday biographical facts – it was, she confessed, 'a most difficult thing for a writer of fiction' to stick to documentary accuracy – but here, at last, was a story that needed no embroidery to give it a sensationally novelistic spin.

Gaskell's new-found knowledge, however, put her in a difficult position. Her work in progress was conceived as an apologia, not as an exposé. At the time of Brontë's death the previous year, her public image had been dubious, her novels attacked as unladylike and sexually 'coarse'. Gaskell's aim was to save her friend and fellow-novelist's reputation by recreating her as a tragic heroine with unimpeachable morals. She wanted to show the 'thoughtless' critics, who had cast such aspersions, that the author of *Jane Eyre* was not 'susceptible' to the 'passion of love'.

It was impossible, in the circumstances, for Gaskell to do anything other than suppress what she had learnt about her subject's feelings for the professor. In the finished biography, she would quote only a few innocuous passages from the letters, glossing over Charlotte's relationship with Heger and hyping up the story of Branwell Brontë's adulterous love affair in an act of biographical displacement. Yet, as Gaskell well knew, while the documents were in existence they represented a ticking time bomb, capable of blowing Charlotte Brontë's reputation apart. 'I can not tell you how I should deprecate anything leading to the publication of those letters,' she told her publisher George Smith on 1 August 1856.

Gaskell's *Life of Charlotte Brontë*, published in 1857, was a triumph of hagiographic image management. It succeeded beyond all hope in transforming perceptions of its subject, enshrining her in the public mind as a 'valiant heroine made perfect by sufferings'. The dangerous letters, however, continued to survive, shut up in Madame Heger's jewel box.

For two decades they remained there untouched, with Charlotte's secret known only to Monsieur and Madame Heger. The next person to see them was the Hegers' daughter Louise. Attending a literary lecture, she was horrified to hear her parents denounced for their cold and inhuman treatment of the great novelist Charlotte Brontë while she was under their roof. When she asked her mother for an explanation, Madame Heger showed her the letters. She then locked them up again with her jewels.

Louise clearly kept her counsel. But after her mother died in 1890, she confronted her father with the letters. Irritated and surprised, he responded by throwing them in the bin, just as he had 45 years previously. Amazingly, they survived this second disposal attempt, rescued this time by Louise. But when her father died nearly 20 years later, she showed them to her brother Paul who realized their importance as literary documents and eventually made the momentous decision to make them public and donate them to the British Library.

On 29 July 1913, an English translation of the letters was printed in *The Times*. The result was as explosive as Mrs Gaskell had feared. Panic ensued among those who saw themselves as the guardians of Charlotte's reputation, such as the journalist and Brontë expert Clement Shorter. Blustering his way through, he denied that there was anything improper in the letters. They merely expressed, he said, the affectionate respect one would expect from a young pupil to a teacher double her age. Oddly, Shorter's expertise on the Brontës seemed to desert him. In fact, the age difference between the mature student in her 20s and the young, saturnine professor had been a mere seven years.

Feminists also took fright at the evidence that Charlotte had been in love with a married man. The novelist and Brontë biographer May Sinclair had so longed for her idol to be a 'virgin priestess of art' that, according to her protegée Rebecca West, the revelation distressed her as much as a personal bereavement. The image of angelic purity that Gaskell had so carefully created had been once and for all dispelled.

The real Charlotte Brontë, it seems, had finally become visible. Yet had she? Rather than giving new complexity to her popular image, the publication of the letters would have the uncomfortable effect of creating a new but equally limited caricature, reworking her as a pulsating romantic heroine in the Mills and Boon mode. The 1940s biopic, *Devotion*, had Heger as an absurd French roué taking a coquettish Charlotte to the local funfair to teach her a thing or two in the tunnel of love. Even the respected biographer Winifred Gérin produced a sentimental play, *My Dear Master* (1955), which, according to a review, 'rose no higher than a women's magazine serial'.

As I sat in the British Library, examining the Heger letters through their protective glass covers, I tried to tell myself that it was like looking through a window into the writer's soul. Yet perhaps because I couldn't touch them, I felt a nagging sense that I was deceiving myself, that the intimacy they appeared to offer was delusive. I even caught myself wondering whether the letters' continued existence had actually limited the appreciation of Charlotte Brontë's works by encouraging overly biographical interpretation, particularly of her masterpiece *Villette*, whose sophisticated exploration of psychology makes it far deeper than a *roman à clef*.

The letters may seem to offer up the 'truth', but their meaning is in fact more fugitive than that. Unlike straightforward love letters, their tone is shifting and unstable. Sometimes Charlotte writes at a pitch of soul-baring intensity, but at other times she adopts the polite tone of the respectful student. Elsewhere, she seems to be calculatedly creating literary scenarios on the page, as if translating her life into a novel. In other places, the letters seem to be more about her own, agonized ambitions as a writer than about the man she is addressing.

The four letters, in addition, are only part of a larger picture which does not survive in full. There may have been other letters from Charlotte, now missing; and as Heger's own side of the correspondence is absent, it is hard to reconstruct his exact role in the relationship. To what extent did he invite her emotional attachment? To what extent, if at all, was he attracted to her? The role of his wife is even harder to pin down. What did she think she had to gain by painstakingly stitching together the fragments she found in the wastepaper basket? Was she gathering evidence that her husband was a sexual harasser of students? Or did she want evidence, if it were needed in the future, that Mademoiselle Charlotte had been a crazy stalker?

In the end, the letters raise more questions than they answer. You can look at them through the glass, but the fact that you cannot handle them keeps them, symbolically, out of reach. The tears that run across them make me think of Virginia Woolf's comment that what biography does is to 'tack together torn bits of stuff, stuff with raw edges'. However much evidence the biographer pulls together, there will always be gaps between the reassembled pieces. Fissures will always remain in our pictures of past lives. The written documents left behind by the dead are not like photographic plates after all; they refuse to be developed into a clear-cut positive image. Patchwork, rather than photographic likeness, is all the biographer can truly hope to achieve.

John Sutherland

No Respect

I became a biographer (not, incidentally, what is written as 'occupation' on my passport) out of motives of low idealism. Three such motives, to be precise.

The first was that, as a serving academic, my discipline has – over the years – run away from me. More precisely, I can't keep up with it. The reason, obviously, is 'theory'. I find it so hard to follow learned discourse in the journals and cutting edge monographs that I must either doubt my abilities (very lowering to the morale), or despise my colleagues for expending their intellect into what is, effectively, a wasteland of cleverness. The subject, in short, has become hieratic.

Linked to this first reason is the shrinking market for academic literary criticism. Many of the more distinguished imprints have backed out from publishing it – too many writers (every academic seeking tenure in the US, and promotion in the UK), too few readers; above all, too few purchasers. And – with the erosion of library acquisition budgets (nothing easier to cut when times are hard) – the institutional sale has slumped. And, of course, the fewer (sold) the higher (the discourse). Too high for me; or, if I'm honest, too much effort required to reach up there.

Biography has obvious attractions to the academic recoiling from the latest mutations in literary criticism. It is, if well done, intellectually respectable. Nor does one have to agonize about how to do it. There is, in biography, a 'script' already written. Literary remains await. The life is there, you follow it, birth to grave, with whatever digressions and grace notes you can bring to it. Most importantly, there is someone to write for. Many someones. Although, as publishers gloomily protest, 'the vogue for literary biography has passed' (no more Ackroyd-Holroyd seven-figure advances) there remains, nonetheless, a solid and substantial readership, if you can reach it. People, that is, who want what you've got. In my local Waterstones (by University College London) the 'Literature' section has shrunk and receded over the years. It's now in the bookstore equivalent of Siberia – up the stairs, at the back. 'Biography' holds its place, prominently, on the ground floor.

Most attractively for biographers like myself, the readership for the commodity (if well done) is both inside and outside the academic borders. A biography, that is to say, can hope to get into the 'General Trade' lists, beyond the contracting pale of the 'Literature' ghetto. It connects (fine Forsterian thought) with the common reader (fine Johnsonian and Woolfian concept).

It is not mere opportunism, or commercialism, to bridge this gap (gulf as it has become) between specialist scholarship and lay (but intelligent) readership. The crossover market is something that academics too seldom take note of. Dickens, for example, figures in all respectable English Department curricula and probably sells, I would guess, about 20,000 copies a year of his novels to students. But he sells 200 times as many (through the classic reprint lines) to readers who are not – and may never have been – students. When, in 2005, the BBC-Andrew Davies TV version of *Bleak House* goes out, it will (on Davies's previous form) attract a viewing audience of five-million plus.

A biography of Dickens (such as Ackroyd's, Fred Kaplan's, or Michael Slater's, which is on its way) will, proportionately, sell in the tens of thousands. An academic monograph on, say, 'extradiegetic strategies in *Bleak House*' will do well to break into the low hundreds before hitting the remainder table and then the pulping press. The tie-in edition of the novel will, while the series is running, sell many hundreds of thousands. Who is serving Dickens better?

The third attraction of biography is also linked to market. High levels of readership means respectable levels of payment. Scholarship well done is its own reward – particularly if it earns the applause of one's peers. But money is also sweet. And reassuring. Like other labourers, the scholar should be worthy of his hire.

That being said, biography does not rate high in academic circles. The Research Assessment Panels tend to be only moderately impressed. And biography draws the same, often unstated, objection as does higher journalism: 'Anyone could do it: I could do it, if I bothered to.' It's wrong, of course. But biography is, sadly, something of a 'no respect' kind of scholarship in the university: higher, probably, than 'editing', but lower than the monograph.

I have written three biographies: of Mrs Humphry Ward, of Sir Walter Scott and, most recently, of Sir Stephen Spender. My experience, for what it is, has taught me that 'subject' is everything. It is not, unfortunately, the case that an interesting subject will, by itself, interest the primary purchaser (the publisher). I would, for example, dearly like to write the life of William Sharp (1855–1905), the uptight Victorian novelist whose alter ego was the untutored Scottish genius, Fiona MacLeod. The transgender games Sharp played are amazing (he wrote, for example, a *Who's Who* entry for his Celtic 'cousin' separate from his own). The doubly authored fiction is good and there is a tempting quantity of unexploited archive material to draw on. But there is, alas, no 'name recognition' for either Sharp or MacLeod. Offer to write the umpteenth biography of Dickens, Jane Austen, or Hardy and it will, probably, be snapped up, if you have a good track record as a biographer. Offer Sharp-MacLeod (as I have) and the response will be polite indifference.

If you want to write the biography of a subject who will yield a six-figure advance (not unreasonable in biography – a field in which research can be extremely expensive) you will probably need diplomatic skills (to deal with the estate) and a good agent to handle the competition. My bid to write the authorized life of Spender was fortified by the fact that I had been his colleague. But getting the assignment was the result of complex negotiation over many months. And selling the project at auction was similarly fraught. Actually doing the biography was something of a relief, after the ardours of the deal.

Where large advances are involved, there will be other professional biographers chasing the best subjects. Rivalry is sharp and so, sometimes, is practice. There are, of course, many other good subjects whose lives are worthy of book-length commemoration. But for them sales are likely to be respectable and the royalties will not be enough to live on. Of course, academics have their salaries. But, as I say, biography is not something that can be done by ratiocination in a cork-lined room. It will probably require travel, permission fees, and a lot of expensive library work in inconvenient places. Even academics, cushioned by their salaries, will need some supplementary support (grant and fellowship awarding bodies tend to have, like the RAE, a sadly low opinion of the biographer: it's not impossibly hard to get hand-outs from, say, the British Academy or Leverhulme. The Harry Ransom Center, by contrast, is very generous – but it's in Texas).

The ego rewards of writing biography are considerable. They tend to be noticed. Editors like to review biographies, because of the human interest. Booksellers display them. Publishers like to give them nice covers. And biography, for the author, offers that peculiar sensation which I, personally, have only experienced when acting on stage. That is to say, once you are well embarked into the project you feel you are 'inside' your subject. You know him or her, almost as well as they know themselves (and, of course, you know what they don't – what will happen next). This inwardness is particularly the case (as it commonly is with literary biography) if the narrative draws on private correspondence, journals and other personal materials – things never meant for a stranger's eye. One feels (the analogy is irresistible) godlike. Until, that is, the reviews and the royalties come in.

I'm between biographies and looking for a subject. I'd like to do Michael Stipe (lead singer of REM and, in my opinion, a distinguished poet-lyricist) but he hasn't replied to my letters. It may have to be William Sharp. Or Fiona MacLeod.

Kathryn Hughes

Fever

During my apprentice years as a biographer, I could never quite understand this business of literary haunting. Writers much more experienced than I would appear in the press talking half-mournfully, half-ecstatically about the way in which their subjects regularly took over their lives. To hear them speak you would imagine that Catullus, Byron and Virginia Woolf were mostly to be found lounging round a Highbury kitchen, shoes kicked off, glass of Pinot Grigio in hand, waiting until their biographer emerged from their study ready for an evening of glorious reminiscence and high-quality literary chat.

For me it was never like that. My subjects did not take over my life. Indeed, I made sure that they knew their place, which was not in my head but in my computer, where they were obliged to stay until I commenced work at 8 o'clock sharp the next morning. I did not encourage fraternizing, day-dreaming or speculation. 'Footstepping' – the practice of folding your own life into your subject's in order to get closer to him – had never worked for me. I had spent many chilly hours standing in historic houses and churchyards trying to force a fellow-feeling that stubbornly refused to come. This was often because there were nearly always other people present who insisted unwittingly on breaking the spell. One dreamy visit to a reconstructed Victorian schoolroom for a book I was writing on governesses ended abruptly when one little girl whispered loudly, 'Mummy, what's that lady *for*?'

But halfway through my last book, a biography of George Eliot, something changed. I finally began to understand what all those seasoned biographers had been writing about all along. I'm not talking here simply about the writerly madness that comes from spending too much time on your own, in pyjamas, so that when you finally emerge blinking for a quick dash to the shops you become convinced that the police car on the corner has been staking out your house prior to arresting you for a crime so heinous that you can't even begin to think what it might be. I mean more the growing conviction that comes over biographers that their subjects have chosen them to tell their story (rather than the other way round) and are sending them uncanny messages from beyond the grave.

When I embarked on the George Eliot biography ten years ago I loved her work but knew little of her life. Within the first few months of research I discovered that as a young woman Eliot had been a frequent visitor to the unremarkable east London square where I live: a house I can see from my window happened to be the home of her best friend. A year into the project I was showing my then boyfriend photographs of the building in the Strand where Eliot had boarded and worked for several years when he suddenly announced that for most of the twentieth century the place had actually belonged to his family.

A non-biographer might see nothing strange here – in social and cultural terms Victorian London was a smaller place than it is today, with the same groups of busy, clever people popping up in different contexts all the time. But to me it was a sign that I had been uniquely chosen to write this book. Oh, all right then, to show you how mad I had actually become, I thought that *Eliot herself* had chosen me to write the book and was sending me encouraging little prods from beyond the grave to let me know that she was happy with her choice and the way that my work was going.

It gets madder, though. About four years into the Eliot project my 8-year-old godson asked me why I was 'talking funny'.

By this I don't think Joe meant that I had suddenly adopted Eliot's carefully poshed-up Nuneaton accent. It was more that my sentences had become extraordinarily long, full of qualifying phrases, inflected with a knowing resignation about the folly of the human race combined with a tender affection for its basic, silly goodness. Joe, though, just found it tedious to wait while I meandered through a long, thoughtful disquisition on human appetite when all he'd asked for was a glass of Sunny D.

The moment the Eliot book was published, I was free from her haunting. She was no longer there when I woke up in the morning, sitting at the end of my bed nodding and smiling gently with encouragement. She no longer hovered over my shoulder looking at the VDU screen as I typed away. My speech even reverted to its usual jerky, fractured pattern and I found that, to be quite honest, I couldn't care less about suffering humanity and the pickle into which it had got itself. All I wanted to do was have fun – a particularly un-Eliot type concept.

I still feel slightly queasy coming clean about my biographical fever, with its hallucinations and manic grandiosity. It seems so shaming, exactly the kind of sentimental approach that the scrupulous scholar must take care to avoid. The end result, otherwise, is a kind of narcissistic identification with one's subject which can lead to some truly awful blunders. (No one, surely, wants to be accused of writing perennially about themselves – that is what we have Autobiography for.) But I think now that, used properly, this fever must be a good thing. For without that central, pulsing madness, how else could anyone give up five years of their life to living with an imaginary friend whom only they can see?

Ann Wroe

Caught in the Net

What could be better than embarking on a life that has never been done before? It is like walking out into a field of virgin snow: no one has yet trampled it, and the only tracks will be your own.

But some lives have never been written for good reason. And when I approached the life of 'Perkin Warbeck', who laid claim to the throne of England at the end of the fifteenth century, I knew I faced the most fundamental obstacle of all. We still do not know who this young man was; and, what is more, we may never know.

He said he was Richard, Duke of York, the younger of the princes in the Tower. Much of the evidence, not least his looks and manners, suggests this may have been so. On his capture by Henry VII in 1497, he agreed that he was actually Perkin Warbeck, the son of a Tournai boatman; but he did not behave as though he believed it, and neither did Henry. On the other hand, his story of his 'survival' was always thin, and the idea that the princes escaped violent death is as hard to credit now as it was then. The scales of probability shift constantly, first one way and then the other.

Even as I started, I knew that to try to write his life was more likely to deepen the mystery than to solve it. It is the tiny details of his career that throw up the inconsistencies, the mysteries, the inexplicable behaviour of both enemies and friends, and the whiff of very old cover stories. To write his life would be relatively easy if, like everyone before me, I was prepared to call him 'Warbeck' or 'Richard' from the first, and take it on from there.

But I knew I could not, and must not, base a whole book on either assumption.

So what then? Highmindedness is all very well; but biographers need to know where a life starts in order to begin the task. Whatever we believe about nature or nurture, our birth and upbringing have an effect both on what we are, and on what we become. Yet the alternative beginnings of this young man were as far apart as could be imagined. If he was Richard, my subject had been born in an English palace and raised as a prince; if he was Perkin, he had been born into the roughest, poorest part of Tournai, and brought up on the docks. If he was the prince, his long, hopeless struggle to reclaim his kingdom was a tragedy of desertion by his own people; if he was the boatman's boy, it was an adventure which, at its highest point, led him to undreamt-of heights of opulence, celebrity and love.

My biography, I began to realize, would have to write both stories. It would also have to leave open a third possibility: that he was neither the boatman's boy nor the prince, but someone else entirely, to whom the extraordinary track of his life would have looked different again. I was dealing, of course, with only one person – one soul, as I thought of him – whose charming, clever and timorous character emerged clearly from the evidence. But from time to time, and from place to place, his various identities cast him in quite different lights. Nor were these merely the identities others gave him, for it seems that, by the end, even he was no longer certain who he was.

If he had no fixed identity, it was also impossible to name him. He was 'Richard' or 'York' to his supporters, 'Perkin' or 'the feigned lad' to Henry and his men; that much was easy. But what was he to me? When I wanted to mention him myself, I would have to find unloaded terms: 'the young man', 'Henry's prisoner', 'her protégé', 'her husband'. I would have to do the same in the index, in which, of course, he could not appear. Rather than explain these extraordinary qualms to anyone else, I did the index myself, wishing my fate had been otherwise.

In general, however, my fate enthralled me. I had a subject who was going to force me to break the bounds of biography; someone whose life could not be narrated in a straight line from A to Z. If this was slightly worrying, it was also profoundly liberating. Walking one day on Hampstead Heath, where most of my book-thinking gets done, I told myself: 'This is a book about seeing.' My themes would be perception, deception and illusion, all related to one young man at one particular point in history. I could retail all the facts, but I would also have to lay out the mists and uncertainties; and readers themselves would have to be the judges, as if they too walked beside this glittering figure in the 1490s, trying to work out who he was.

Once the theme and structure were there – apparently confirmed by the wind, the sky and the trees – I would not have changed it for the world. I was running a little ahead of myself, for I was still doing the research. But even supposing I found the answer to the mystery, I still wanted to approach it in the same fashion: obliquely, variously, by shifting lights, trying to pin down my subject in fifteenth-century ways. There was an added advantage to this, that it helped to flesh out the tiny fragments of evidence about him. If I could place him in a panorama of the time, physical, mental and moral, it would matter less that we have only three scraps of his conversation, two letters, a portrait, a will and a bundle of largely faked 'confessions'. He would live in his world like a flickering thought, an imminence as much as a presence, the very 'imp' and 'butterfly' he appeared to his contemporaries.

Only once did my resolve waver. Predictably, it happened when I thought I had solved the mystery. It was late in the day, in every sense; I had written the first draft already. I was in Brussels, where I had come to research one character in particular: a little boy called Jehan le Sage, who had been taken in in 1478 by Margaret of York, Duchess of Burgundy, the main driving force behind the Yorkist plots of the 1490s. I already knew that, intriguingly, he was exactly the same age as Richard of York (though Richard was then still alive and thriving in England). I knew, too, that the boy had been hidden away in the palace of Binche in Hainault. For Margaret, who had no children, Jehan was a cherished surrogate son. The Binche estate accounts, in which I was immersed, painted a brief but compelling picture of this child: in effect, a little prince, beautifully dressed and carefully educated. And they told me that in 1485, the year when Yorkist hopes died at Bosworth, he and his tutor had disappeared.

Was this the boy who was to reappear, six years later, as 'Richard'? After two days of tracking him, I felt I could not go home until I had answered the question. When the archives closed I sat on a bench in the park, wet November leaves fluttering round me in the dusk, and watched the Bruxellois walk their dogs up and down the sanded paths. Surely the answer was yes, wasn't it? Part of me held back, as usual, scribbling down doubts on a piece of paper; the other part, like a Pekinese wildly straining on the leash, longed to plunge headlong into certainty.

The next day tested me even more severely. I was back in the archives, or rather in the school gym that had become the temporary archives, as the murky afternoon drew in. The room was crowded, as it always was, and noisy with both French and Flemish. The two language groups had different document-fetchers, both obstreperous and sulky; the Fleming, big and blond, smoked in his corner, and readers ate rolls stuffed with sausage at their desks.

The Binche accounts were now offering page after page of plumbing and carpentry expenses, in one continuous block of script. Perhaps I could skip this; I was in 1496, with my boy long gone, and I felt tired. But then a word leapt out of the page: *Richard*. In this context, in Hainault, it was a foreign name; I had never seen it in these accounts before. The entry concerned a room under the chapel with the tennis court outside. Margaret was setting up this room as a shrine, with a traverse screen, new latticed windows and a papal candle in a special stand; and she had renamed it *la chambre de Richart*, 'Richard's room'. But this was also the room in which Jehan had lived, years before, when Margaret had kept him at the palace.

Very seldom do archive entries cause a real shock to the heart. This one could only refer to the 'Richard', Margaret's great hope, who was then at the court of Scotland, preparing to invade England – or to his little son, also Richard, who was born that year. And surely that particular room was dedicated to him because, in times past, it had been his?

For the rest of the day, 'Richard's room' dinned in my head like a bell that would not stop. Because I was staying with Polish friends, I went that evening to a concert of music from the Tatra mountains; in the midst of the frantic dancing and fiddle-playing, 'Richard's room' was all I could think of. I knew something no one else in the hall knew, no one else in the world knew, a fact whose significance no one else had grasped. Perhaps I now had a place in which to start his childhood, at least: in an ambiance of Margaret's love, which would have continued to inspire both the boy's career and her own ambitions. My heart flew; everything made sense.

Yet could I truly start there? I still had no idea where this child had come from, and again the path forked: he was either an English royal bastard (strange snippets in Edward IV's warrants for issues suggested that might be so), or he was an orphan from somewhere in the Burgundian territories; or perhaps, since 'Perkin's' supposed father was a violent criminal, he had been sent away from Tournai and taken into care. This life was never going to be straightforward unless I manhandled the truth into one template or another; and I was already committed to a far more delicate operation. In the end, the story of Margaret's little boy was kept for the final pages where, I hoped, it would strike people as it had struck me, with the full force of a possibility which had never before been considered. Up to that point – and maybe beyond it – the book could only be a tentative journey into the secrets of a soul.

I would never have written a biography of Gladstone this way. There may be only one case – 'Perkin's' case – in which the evidence of identity is so ambiguous that new ways are needed to catch him. And though in my head I still have no name for him, I felt in the end that he was there, fluttering, timid and beautiful, in the mesh of my net.

Michael Holroyd

Finding a Good Woman

Is it desirable, or even legitimate, for writers to cross gender lines? I have been authoritatively told by some strict scholars that men should not make women the subjects of their biographies. An example of this encroachment, often cited, is Virginia Woolf. Her biographer Quentin Bell presented her as someone wholly without a political mind; while Hermione Lee and other women have since revealed her to be a powerful and committed political writer. This represents more than different definitions of what makes up politics. Men, it is said, inevitably keep women in the historical compartments from which all their lives they have struggled to escape.

Whenever I am asked why I have never written about a woman I reply that I have done so frequently and will continue to do so. I have handed over many pages, even chapters, in my books to women: to Carrington in my *Lytton Strachey*; to Gwen and Ida John in my *Augustus John*; and to Charlotte Payne-Townshend, Erica Cotterill, Beatrice Webb and others in my *Bernard Shaw*. In various autobiographical writings I have also written a good deal about my mother and my aunt. I like, as it were, putting the pen into the hands of women, but it is true that no woman's name has yet appeared on my title pages.

Several times I seemed to be heading in that direction. Early in my career Jacqueline du Pré tentatively sounded me out as to whether I would write her life. By then she was suffering from multiple sclerosis. Her plan was to speak into a tape; I would then listen to it, ask her questions and, helped by mutual friends, we would proceed with the dialogue until we had assembled a

collaborative draft, much of which could be reshaped as narrative. But I could not see how this technique would work for
anything beyond a magazine article. Besides, to write the life of a
living person is to enter a minefield, while skirting safely around
the edges seems a tepid business, unsatisfactory and inadequate.

A rather different proposal came from Doris Lessing who
invited me to write her biography after her death. We were
travelling through China at the time and later, as the years progressed and Doris went from strength to strength, bringing out
two fine volumes of autobiography and introducing some semi-
autobiographical passages into her fiction, so our agreement,
departing into the distance, seemed increasingly surreal. Nevertheless she has employed me during this period as a shield
against those whom she positively wished to prevent writing
books about her. So I have had my uses. As to the book itself, I
think it will probably turn out to be a work of the imagination –
that is, a posthumous work for both of us.

Ideas for writing about extraordinary, if rather obscure, women
have frequently attracted me – for example Gertrude Caton-
Thompson. She was an intrepid, early twentieth-century
archaeologist who described her chief recreation as 'idleness' and
who, as if to illustrate this, would sometimes go to sleep in empty
tombs with, it was said, 'cobras for company and a pistol under
her pillow to ward off prowling hyenas'. She had spent part of
her childhood in Maidenhead near where I lived as a child with
my grandparents, and had actually gone to school at a house in
Eastbourne where my grandfather lived with his father when a
boy. But could I follow her from such soft English country over
the seas and into the Sahara, then off to the monumental ruins in
Zimbabwe where she worked, and to the mysterious Moon
Temple in Arabia? These were alluring destinations, but I
eventually decided that Gertude Caton-Thompson's passion for

pre-history and my own more present interests were too far removed from one another.

Invitations to write biographies of women (Pamela Hansford Johnson was another) have always come at impossible moments – that is, after I have already begun a biography of some bearded man. But one woman haunted me for a long time and I kept returning to her until I had a cupboard full of fading and dusty papers about her, waiting in a dark corner of my room. They are waiting there still.

I came across her by accident. My original plan has been to write about Gabrielle Enthoven, a mysterious bisexual woman whose passion for the theatre had led to the creation of the Theatre Museum in London. In its early days, like a circus, the museum was forever on the move from place to place – various respectable institutions fighting hard to avoid the honour of housing it. When I started looking at the Enthoven papers, they had left Leighton House and come to settle temporarily at the Victoria and Albert Museum before travelling on to Covent Garden. Its director was Alexander Schouvaloff, a legendary, aristocratic figure with gleaming shoes, thick black hair brushed across his forehead, and dark eyes which narrowed dramatically whenever you spoke to him. It was rumoured that he had been recruited by Roy Strong but then had fallen out with him – and to such a degree that, in the Pushkin manner, he felt obliged to challenge Roy Strong to a duel. Perhaps mercifully, he was seldom encountered by visitors to the collection, and the people I met were the deputy director Jennifer Aylmer, an eager, grey-haired woman with bright pink lipstick who came from a well-known theatre family, and her assistant, a brilliant-looking young girl who quite dazzled me.

Apparently it is not the way of scholars to pay any attention to an assistant's assistant. 'I was flattered that you noticed me,' she later told me. But how could anyone fail to notice her? She was what the Pre-Raphaelites used to call 'a stunner'. My difficulty lay in keeping my eyes and mind on Gabrielle Enthoven's piles of playbills which lay in the shade when, having deposited them with me, she left on some other scholarly errand. I remember that when I signed the visitors' book on the desk, she asked me what I was studying. I explained what I thought I was doing and she brought me some material that was not yet catalogued. I was apparently so fascinated by it that I stayed until closing time – after which we went out for a drink together.

Though my interest in these playbills and programmes waned over the following weeks, I often used to go to the Victoria and Albert Museum. My new girl friend usually worked late and I would wait for her after the public had left, wandering through the empty galleries and halls. It was during these wanderings that I came across Rodin's extraordinary bust of Eve Fairfax.

It had been commissioned in 1902 by her fiancé, Ernest William Beckett, later the second Lord Grimthorpe, when she was in her late 20s. But the bust was never paid for and the engagement broken off. Whatever happened remained a mystery, though there were many dark rumours, I discovered, involving bankruptcy and an illegitimate child. Her face continued to fascinate me – it always seemed to have changed when I returned to look at her. But she kept her secrets well and eventually I decided that she had dipped so far below the horizon that I could not reach or write about her. Only later did I find out that she was still alive at that time – she died in York in 1978, destitute and unmarried, in her 107th year.

Eve Fairfax has been a biographical tease. Every time I pursue her she retreats into the mists of legend, but when I give up the chase, some letters, the account of an adventure or a strange birth certificate arrives in the post. So I have decided to ignore her in the hope that she will pursue me.

Meanwhile what papers I have gathered continue to fade under a layer of dust. Some scholars may be pleased that I am not actively seeking to cross the gender line. But I would like to do so, believing those 'Do Not Trespass' notices are already somewhat out of date. Surely, I would argue, there is room for, say, Nina Auerbach's stimulating, feminist life of Ellen Terry and for the authoritative theatre biography of her by Roger Manvell – the existence of both enriches the practice of biography. The truth is that although I am not dogmatically opposed to ideologically motivated lives, I tend to favour some cross-dressing and find myself looking forward to reading the new life of Leonard Woolf by Victoria Glendinning.

Ben Pimlott

Brushstrokes

Biography has come a long way. In particular, it can claim to be as ancient as any other written form – poetry, for instance, with which it is inextricably linked. It has also been powerfully influential. Most of the world's great religions have a biographical element: at the core of Christian teaching are four resonant biographies.

Biography has had its ups and downs over the last few millennia, but today – ostensibly – we live in a biographical golden age. No literary genre is more sought after. Many upper-brow members of the public, when asked what they read, say 'Biographies' without being very specific about subject area. The well-researched life seems to have an appeal to people who are made impatient by mere fiction: perhaps it is protestant self-improvement and voyeurism wrapped into one. That biography is popular, however, is beyond dispute.

Yet biography's position remains uneasy. There is a kind of person that sneers at biography. There are several reasons for this. The most obvious is that many biographies do not live up to the claims made for them. Because publishers, newspapers, agents are enthusiastic about biography, many writers – novelists, say, or poets with little biographical talent – try their hand, with embarrassing results. Hence biography has a mixed reputation among writers and critics who have not, themselves, joined the goldrush and who claim that many biographies are badly written, factually sloppy and hagiographical. At the same time, there is a philosophical objection.

The harder objection to deal with is the philosophical one. 'Creative' writers and analytic historians maintain that biography is neither chalk nor cheese: limited in imaginative range, and of its nature insufficiently grounded in the historical method. More than 40 years have elapsed since E. H. Carr issued his classic and super-ficially persuasive denunciation of biography in *What is History?* Meanwhile there have been others in the Cambridge radical tradi-tion who have been similarly scornful. Eric Hobsbawm dismisses them as 'Victorian tomes'. Provocative echoes of this are to be found in the essays of David Cannadine. At the same time, the literary establishment, with powerful English faculty professors as its gatekeepers, has woken up to the role of biography, but draws an unspoken distinction – treating 'biography' and 'literary biog-raphy' (i.e. biographies of writers) as synonymous terms, and often ignoring non-literary biography altogether. Thus there is a growing academic literature on 'biography' that takes no account of the biographies of scientists or statesmen.

In a way, this prejudice – conscious and often unconscious – is odd, and not just because many of those who deride biographies nevertheless read them. It cannot be dismissed as merely snobbish; neither is it just the product of a progressive movement in favour of emphasizing social movements over 'chaps' – the old-fashioned stress on the role of the individuals. The simple sociology-mindedness of one school of history has long been dis-placed, in our so-called postmodern world, by a greater tolerance of variety. Probably, it was never philosophical at all, but merely reflected the sad reality that most of the talked-about biographies lacked the qualities of imaginative insight and rigour available in other disciplines; and the number of biographies worth reading for their own sake, rather than for the information conveyed, was and remains small.

Are there as many low-quality novels and history books? Possibly. It could be, however, that one reason for resentment is that biography has an unfair advantage. Where a novelist has to create a world and grab attention within the first few pages, a biographer can compensate for dull thoughts and flat writing by offering a stolen yarn about a figure of historical interest. A second reason is more generic. Sometimes, the popularity of a product leads to change. At other times, it has the opposite effect. Publishers and agents join together: if this is what the public likes, let them have more of it – and that is what is supplied. Hence one cause of irritation about biography in the hands of many earnest practitioners is that it has become a constipated form. Ever longer, ever better-researched biographies are becoming scholarly monuments – to be admired and surreptitiously skimmed, rather than read *in toto* as cohesive works of art. The modern biographer with ambition (and, probably, an academic career) likes to be 'definitive', which tends to mean inclusiveness rather than selectivity: a definitive biography is seldom a short one.

So much for the coolness which encourages serious intellectuals to place biography on the fringes of historical or critical writing. Since the earliest Hittite and Chinese inscriptions, and more particularly since Plutarch, writing about the lives of heroes and villains has passed restlessly through many phases. It is fair to believe that it will last at least as long as the parvenu novel. But where is it heading?

Of course the accusation of immobility is not to denigrate biography as such, or even many of the books in the dock. On the contrary: few would dispute that the boom of the last 20 years has done an enormous amount for the quality of biographies, or that the best half-dozen published each year compare favourably with all but a handful of star volumes published a generation ago. Both the scholarship and scholarly apparatus of the contemporary study of a life have improved beyond measure, and some of the old gripes – about purple passages in which the author attempts to read the subject's mind – have largely been disposed of by a cohort of new biographers who have no truck with anything but source-based data.

This is all to the good. What is not so good is the formulaic nature of even the best of contemporary biographical writing, the tight defensiveness of the genre in the face of the kind of criticisms mentioned, and the lack of experimentation. There are a few wild cards, playing around with chronology. Some writers have tried group biography. None, however, has yet succeeded in becoming an effective revolutionary, or has made a particularly convincing attempt to do so. Indeed, there is a strong argument for saying that, despite Lytton Strachey and a century of supposed biographical iconoclasm, the Victorian tome still reigns. Most biographies are as explicit as possible about private peccadilloes. But almost all remain judgemental, seeing as a key objective the enchantment of the subject's reputation. This is particularly true of literary biography. Indeed, the conscious or unconscious subtext of virtually all literary biography is that such-and-such hitherto obscure playwright can be excused philandering or domestic violence or other departures from bourgeois moral norms, because of the value of the work.

And so it goes on: biographies get fatter, more professional, harder for the struggling would-be life writer to compete with, given the time and stamina required. Indexes, prefaces, references and explanatory notes expand. Care over artwork and cover design increases, along with prices, and desirability as Christmas presents. Will the trend continue indefinitely, as the public pocket gets deeper and the seasonal appetite for big, solid, meticulous non-fiction continues to grow?

Common sense suggests that a change must come. Given the conservatism of the readers and writers of biographies, the change may be gradual. The big biographies will continue, but some of them may become sleeker. Meanwhile, the public focus may already be shifting a little – away from solidarity and towards biographical imagination.

To say this is not to make a nostalgic plea on behalf of the 'evocative' or 'atmospheric' biography, which places intuition above learning. It is more to note an emerging taste for the book about a famous person that does not require 300 pages of references to make its points, but – on the contrary – makes every telling phrase and word count. Roy Jenkins, author of long, brilliant books about Gladstone and Churchill but also of tight essays of selected leaders, comes to mind. So does Francis Wheen's wittily de-mystifying *Karl Marx*. Such books show that the scope, in skilled hands, of biographical writing and the insights it can offer into the human condition are really limitless, and that biography need not regard itself as anybody's poor (or *nouveau riche*) relation.

Neither should biography be seen as a hybrid, occupying an intellectually untenable position between fact-based history and true creative writing. Biography is itself. What a biography ought to be like is of course an unanswerable question, although biography in the modern sense operates within fairly tight rules – attention to accuracy, avoidance of *suppressio veri* most important among them, and a recognition that there is no such thing as a 'true' biography: however scrupulous the research, nobody has access to another's soul, and the character on the page is the author's unique creation. One aspect of the creativity is the subject-in-context and it is this that makes the complaint about over-emphasizing the role of the individual so off-beam. Indeed, far from underplaying social factors, the good biographer highlights them, to give added precision to the story. Good biography is flexible, making unexpected connections across periods of time, and including unexpected essays on topics which, for the involvement of the subject, might never get written about at all.

The metaphor of portraiture is appropriate here. A good biography is like a good portrait: it captures the essence of the sitter by being much more than a likeness. A good portrait is about history, philosophy, milieu. It asks questions as well as answering them, brushstrokes are economical and always to the subtlest effect. Think of Velasquez, Sargent, Freud. Biography can be like that.

Fiona MacCarthy

Baptism by Fire

Perhaps all biographies generate their subplots, secondary personal dramas emitted as a kind of by-product of the enterprise. This was certainly the case with a book I wrote in the late 1980s, a biography of the Catholic craftsman Eric Gill. My subsequent rift with Gill's literary executor, Walter Shewring, contains sadnesses and mysteries still unexplained today.

Shewring was my first contact in planning this biography. As sole literary executor he had the power of permitting or forbidding me to quote from Gill's unpublished correspondence, diaries and other writings, most of which had been sold by Gill's widow Mary to the University of California at Los Angeles after Gill's death in 1940. I knew he had vetoed much of the quotation Malcolm Yorke had hoped to use in his 1981 study of Gill's art, *Eric Gill, Man of Flesh and Spirit*. This meant I approached Shewring, a classical scholar who had been the resident intellectual in the Gills' close circle, with a good deal of trepidation.

For many years he had been a schoolmaster at Ampleforth, the public school attached to the Benedictine monastery in Yorkshire. I sent a tentative letter asking if he could spare an hour or two to see me. He replied back by return in the lovely sub-Gill script I would come to know so well. 'Dear Miss MacCarthy, Certainly I should like to meet you for discussion, but do you know where Ampleforth is?' It was characteristic of Walter to assume potentially disastrous gaps of knowledge in other people's minds. His last instruction too was typical : 'Will you write to let me know? I have a morbid fear of telephones & refuse to answer them.'

I trekked up to Ampleforth on 4 November 1984. Walter was not a monk but he had rooms within the monastery and his life had been celibate – though not from choice, he implied later when our friendship had matured. Being female, I was banned from Ampleforth's monastic heartland, so our interview took place in a barren waiting room warmed only by a very small gas fire of pre-war vintage. Attempting to make this first tea party convivial, Walter had brought along a tin of Scottish shortbread which he opened with some ceremony. He was cautiously approving of the new biography.

I loved him at first sight. Although then in his late 70s, Shewring had something of the freshness of the very clever schoolboy, an irresistible mix of erudition and innocence. A Catholic convert, he had first arrived at Pigotts, Eric Gill's community in the Chilterns, near High Wycombe, in the early 1930s. Like other rootless young men, notably David Jones the painter, the young classicist and poet had been taken in and nurtured. He was still on close terms with Gill's surviving daughter Petra and her children, descending on their families for school holidays from Ampleforth. For me, Walter was important not only in his role as Gill's executor but as a living link with Pigotts, confirming the patterns of its intimate relationships and teaching me its solemn, holy, risqué tone of voice.

We made friends. He sent me copies of his books, made introductions and suggestions, communicating in a peculiar form of speedwriting. Of Gill's former apprentice Michael Richey he informed me 'M.R. is not always accessible, he tends to be intoxicated & foul-mouthed, but if you cd. get hold of him in the right mood, he mt. have some interesting recollections.' The proposed book had become almost a collaboration. By late January 1985 he wrote to ask me what I thought about calling one another by our Christian names, Fiona and Walter, 'without suggestion of an improper intimacy'. He signed the letter 'Yours, Walter (Shewring)', allowing for my possible rejection of the scheme.

Later in that year we met for lunch at a favourite restaurant of Walter's, Marmaduke's Haunted Bistro in York. Walter was in ebullient spirits, having abandoned his old schoolmaster's tweed jacket in favour of a formal three-piece suit and a pinky-mauve wool tie. He ordered two bottles of Corvo wine, his *bon-viveur* side emerging, and talked about Rapallo, Olga Rudge and Ezra Pound. When we left the haunted Bistro, Walter clasped me to him, saying 'Here's to the great book!'

I saw Walter six or seven times over the next two years and we corresponded often. Our meetings settled down into a routine. Sometimes I picked him up from Ampleforth. These northern outings took place on Saturdays. Walter would be waiting outside in the monastery yard clutching a canvas holdall in which to transport back a new supply of very special sherry from his wine merchants in Pickering. Our appointment was for 12 but he always looked as if he had been waiting there since dawn. We would wend our way towards the Pheasant Inn at Harome, returning to Ampleforth late in the afternoon.

When in London, Walter stayed at the Challoner Club, an austere Catholic guest house opposite the Brompton Oratory. Even in the summer he complained that it was freezing. By now accepting my role in providing treats for Walter, I decided to take him to lunch at the Savoy, an environment as diametrically opposed to the rigours of the Challoner as I could devise. Here we ate a whole sole each and Walter was at his most eloquent and charming. Looking back at my old notes of that day's conversation I find the little comment 'I love to talk to him'.

In the summer of 1986 I had spent several weeks studying the Gill collections in the Clark Library at UCLA. It was here, in Gill's diaries, that I found the detailed entries relating not only to his multiple adulterous affairs but also to incest with his sisters and his daughters, and even sexual experiments with the Pigotts dog. In themselves these entries were certainly shocking but somehow they came as a relief to me. My previous half assumptions were now knowledge. Many of the puzzles lingering in Gill's life story were all of a sudden clarified. I knew how to proceed.

The same evidence had been available to Gill's earlier biographer, Robert Speaight, who worked through the same material in preparing his book published in 1966. Speaight, himself a Catholic and a friend of the Gill family, appalled and embarrassed by the revelations, saw it as his duty to suppress them. Twenty years later, the conventions of biography were considerably altered, frank discussion of the sex life of one's subject being well on its way to becoming *de rigueur* for biographers. I did not consider for one moment that Speaight's gentlemanly reticence was possible for me.

Walter had given me his official permission to have photocopies made of Gill material in the States. Once the typescript was finished, in January 1988, I still needed his permission for quotation, especially crucial since the evidence of Gill's sexual aberrations was potentially so explosive and likely to be challenged in Catholic circles where his reputation was still that of revered paterfamilias.

On 23 January, my 47th birthday and a treacherously icy, snowy day, I drove up to Ampleforth to fetch him, having booked a table at the White Swan at Pickering. The typescript was in the boot of the car. After lunch, over coffee, I asked him if I should leave the typescript with him, for perusal at his leisure. He said he would be glad to check the source notes, but as for the text, 'I leave it to you'. The next day he wrote formally in his capacity as Gill's sole literary executor giving me 'unrestricted permission to quote from any unpublished Gill material in any library'.

There is no doubt in my mind that Walter was quite aware of the specific revelations of incest and adultery my typescript would contain. Gill's extreme sexual appetites were no secret to his Pigotts intimates, and Speaight's earlier dilemma in being faced with the same evidence had been the subject of discussion within this inner circle of family and friends.

Walter had himself refused to take on Gill's biography because, he explained, 'I was too fond of Eric'. His reluctance at this juncture to confront the exact contents of my typescript amounted, I believe, to giving it his tacit blessing. He had been fond of Eric but he wanted the truth told so long as he could trust someone else to do the telling. We had been friends for several years, he understood the way I worked and I think he had decided to put his trust in me.

I sometimes wonder if there might have been a further hidden reason, something Walter himself was maybe only half aware of. An element of male jealousy, resentment of Gill's level of sexual charisma and his *droit de seigneur* attitude to sex, emerged in several other interviews with male contemporaries. Walter was now an old man who had spent the majority of his adult life among the monks at Ampleforth. Could his complicity be seen as a final act of protest towards the holy man who flaunted his sexual success?

Through 1988, in the months leading up to publication, there were more excursions, and I met Walter once in Bath on his holiday visit to a Gill descendant. Just before Christmas I sent him an advance copy of the book. He wrote back on 16 January making the general comment, 'Though of course I don't agree with everything that you say, I think you have illuminated a great deal', before launching into two pages of what he called 'school-masterly corrections' on little points of detail. At this stage Walter was still sending me 'much love'.

It was a shock four weeks later to receive another letter, a short distraught note on half a sheet of lined paper which seemed to have been torn out of a school exercise book, telling me that 'our acquaintance & our correspondence must cease'. To me the sense of our collaboration had been precious. I shook with sobs as I read the note, then tore it into strips.

What had happened in the intervening weeks? I can only imagine that members of Gill's family, whose hostility to the book took the form of a bitter personal vendetta towards me, had also turned on Walter and accused him of dereliction of his duty as literary executor. No doubt they had reproached him with being taken in by a sophisticated woman of dubious intentions. Perhaps he had told them of the lunch at the Savoy.

He wrote a few more times, semi-conciliatory letters. After Bernard Levin, at the height of what became a widespread Gill controversy, wrote a vitriolic column in *The Times* accusing me of being too *indulgent* towards Gill, I received a sympathetic letter in a spryly caustic style that was almost the old Walter, defending me against Levin's 'vulgar & mean' attack. But essentially the friendship had now foundered. He died in summer 1990, much enfeebled, his mind wandering, and it was impossible not to suspect that the previous year's painful sequence of events accelerated his decline.

The book on Eric Gill had been my first full-length biography. I began it in a state of naïvety, imagining my only loyalty lay with Gill himself and the truth relating to the bizarre contradictions of this single human life. What I had not been prepared for was the fact that in searching out the truth, especially the truth of a near contemporary, you impinge on other interconnected lives as well, stirring emotions, resurrecting memories. In the dangerous complexities of writing a biography, the book on Eric Gill was my baptism of fire.

D. J. Taylor

He Put My Brother in His Book

Not long ago I took part in a literary festival head-to-head with my fellow-practitioner Midge Gillies, the anatomist of Marie Lloyd and Amy Johnson. During the course of an expert interrogation by a third biographer, Kathryn Hughes, it quickly became clear that Midge and I had radically opposed views of the biographer's art. She, to put it starkly, was a pavement-pounder, a great-moment-re-enactor and a doorstep habitué. I was more of a brood-about-it-in-the-study kind of guy. The audience, I noticed, seemed slightly puzzled by this distinction. What kind of a biographer, you could see them wondering – as I admitted to having seen a signpost to Thackeray's childhood home out on the A303 and declined to follow it – was this? I was unrepentant. It was six hours into an eight-hour drive to Cornwall and the children were growing fractious. In any case, I'd read the letters and seen the drawings, and I *knew* what it would be like.

In writing about W. M. Thackeray (d. 1863) the need to pound pavements and linger on doorsteps was mercifully kept in abeyance. Apart from a few trips to libraries, I could do the work from home, abetted by the six volumes of collected letters and the 26 volumes of the collected works. With George Orwell (d. 1950) on the other hand, it was clear that one was going to have to get out of the house now and again. Consequently I spent several weeks in the Suffolk seaside town of Southwold, where Orwell stayed on and off from the time that his parents retired there late in 1921 to the week of his father's death in August 1939. This was no hardship: Southwold, with its shingly beach and its second-hand bookshops, is my favourite place in the world and the children have long since learned that the correct answer to the whimsical and oft-voiced question, 'Where would Daddy most like to be now?' (usually asked in a car halfway round the M25) is 'On Southwold front in November in the rain.'

Southwold, reconnoitred on dull autumn afternoons with the lights from the Sizewell B nuclear plant five miles down the coast glowing ominously through the mist, offered the chance to ponder several Orwell problems: the identity of the 'backward boy' whom he tutored in nearby Walberswick in the summer of 1930; Dorothy Rogers, the immensely pretty local girl with whose fiancé he came to blows on Southwold Common in 1934; 'Madame Tabois', the town's resident French artist, who had a studio out on the point where the river Blyth flows out to the sea, and from whom Orwell's parents took lessons; Mr Hurst, the borough surveyor, to whom in 1922 Orwell and another disaffected young gentleman from the cramming establishment where both were studying sent the birthday present of a dead rat.

Happily the weeks of loitering in Southwold antique shops and poring over the local phone book – feeling, in fact, like a proper biographer – turned up much that I hadn't bargained for. What I hadn't bargained for in particular was what might be called the 'Southwold attitude' to Orwell. A respectful admiration for the great man who, under his baptismal name of Eric Blair, had wandered intermittently in their midst for nearly two decades? Not a bit of it. Certainly the clutch of 80- and 90-year-olds who had been about in the town in the 1920s and 1930s remembered 'Eric'. On the other hand, he cut so nondescript a figure in the collective imagination that most of the memories were hardly worth putting down on paper. A 'hobo', 'three days away from a shave', come back to the place to sponge off his eminently respectable parents – that was about the extent of bygone Southwold's feeling for Master Blair. The 65 years that had passed since their al fresco set-to had not made George Summers, Miss Rogers's outraged fiancé, now living in nonagenarian Oxfordshire retirement, any less charitable. 'I hated his guts,' he confirmed.

If it comes to that, Orwell hated Southwold, seeing it as a kind of paradigm for everything that he detested about small-town middle England. 'Knype Hill' in his second novel, *A Clergyman's Daughter* (1935), is physically rather closer to Bury St Edmunds – population three times larger and set inland – but there is no mistaking the description of the High Street and the venom that lay beneath it ('one of those sleepy, old-fashioned streets, that look so intensely peaceful on a casual visit and so very different when you live in them and have an enemy or a creditor in every window'). At the same time, though, the town stuck in his head. One fragment, in fact, took as long as a decade to re-emerge.

Quite the oddest interview I conducted among the Southwold cognoscenti was with an old gentleman named George Bumstead. Mr Bumstead, who described himself as a 'recluse', but kept a lively eye on doings in the town, was the son of a grocer with premises at the bottom of the High Street across the road from Montague House, the home of Orwell's parents. As such he remembered lying in bed at night in the early 1930s and listening to the sound of Orwell's typewriter clacking through the evening air. Later, having set up as a grocer himself, he had the pleasure of supplying the Blair seniors (Richard Blair was remembered as a benign but class-conscious old gentleman, capable of sending his tradesman a present on the occasion of his marriage but also cutting him dead if they met in the street on a Sunday).

As I was leaving, Mr Bumstead called me back for a last valediction. 'That George Orwell,' he told me, 'he put my brother in his book.' Which book was that, I wondered? Why, *Nineteen Eighty-Four*. I rushed home, went through it with the proverbial fine-toothcomb, and came finally upon the passage in which Winston Smith, dragged off to the Ministry of Love for interrogation, watches a fellow-prisoner attempt to pass a piece of bread to a man who is clearly starving. 'Bumstead!' roars a voice from the telescreen, '2173 Bumstead J! Let fall that piece of bread!' Jack Bumstead, in other words, the grocer's son from Southwold. Perhaps in the end I shouldn't have been surprised by this carefully hidden signal from a former life. After all, the heroine of *A Clergyman's Daughter*, written at exactly the time that Orwell was coming to blows on Southwold Common with young George Summers, is called Dorothy.

Jenny Uglow

Manuscript Moments

After I have finished a book, accidental insights, the tantalizing gaps, the stories glimpsed out of the corner of my eye, stay in my mind. And often these gaps and finds and tangents are connected with manuscripts.

Since the people I have written about are long dead, I have never held my breath on the verge of discovering a cache of letters or a secret love affair. I haven't had to be tactful, hoping a relative will say 'I'll just see if there is anything in the attic.' Most of the manuscripts that I have used are safely stowed away in libraries, smoothed into letter books and catalogued – carefully or haphazardly. But even so, nothing quite prepares me for the physical sensation of deciphering someone's handwriting, seeing the blots and scratches and sputters where a new pen is needed, the blurring of pencil in hastily written notes and lists, or the way a letter or manuscript of a familiar work scrolls across the page.

I can't forget the day, in the airy light of the Special Collections in the Brotherton Library in Leeds, when I read the manuscript of *Sylvia's Lovers*. It runs on, for page after page, without correction, although Gaskell later went back and scrupulously adjusted her dialect words. Towards the end of each line the writing swoops downwards, as if the author's mind is already two or three words into the next line and her pen is diving to catch up. The impression is less of a writer thinking and composing, than of someone transcribing, dashing to follow the action, frustrated by the slowness of her hand. Turning the pages showed me better than anything how vividly Gaskell saw the imagined scene and how fast her fiction flowed. It made sense of her own advice to a young writer: 'If you think but eagerly of the *story till you see it in action*, words, good, simple words, will come – just as if you saw an accident in the street that impressed you strongly you would describe it forcibly.'

By comparison, the manuscript of her *Life of Charlotte Brontë* is almost comically clotted. It told a different story, of patches and paste and uncomfortable doubts and suppression. Whole lines are crossed through, phrases scored out in dark, thick ink. William Gaskell's neat hand hovers constantly, correcting the grammar. This was a book Gaskell worried about, and not only because of Brontë family pressures or threats of libel. As she burst out ingenuously, knowing all the while that her 'truthful' book was in fact a lie because it hid Charlotte's great secret, her love for Monsieur Heger: 'I never did write a biography, and I don't know exactly how to set about it; you see you have to be accurate and keep to facts; a most difficult thing for a writer of fiction.' Indeed.

The manuscripts speak. I remember, too, opening the small, leather-bound notebook in which William Hogarth scribbled the first draft for *The Analysis of Beauty*. Hogarth, so fast and inventive with the brush and the burin, found words a nightmare. He thought in pictures, with multiple images jostling each other and the linear sequence of prose dismayed him. In common eighteenth-century fashion he folded a page in half, leaving one side free for further thoughts, but halfway through almost every statement, the further thoughts take over, swamping the free left-hand margin, jumping onto the back of the next page, getting tangled with different sections altogether – his unruly ideas simply would not lie down.

Notebooks are almost more evocative than letters. One of my favourites is Erasmus Darwin's garden notebook, its leather cover scuffed and bent from being thrust deep into his greatcoat pocket. He carried it round his garden in Derby, up behind the summerhouse, down to the river, back to the house, noting all the plants, crossing out ones that the frost or slugs had taken. Holding the notebook and seeing how it had been carried around and left out in all weathers, conjured an aspect of this great, stout, exuberant man, that I might not otherwise have glimpsed.

Sifting through manuscripts always reminds me how chance has played its part in dictating what we write. When researching *The Lunar Men*, I was awed by the luck by which Josiah Wedgwood's letters to his partner Thomas Bentley were rescued after they had been sold as waste paper, while a house fire in 1845 meant that all the papers of the chemist James Keir went up in smoke for ever. And whereas Matthew Boulton and James Watt wrote to each other daily when apart, on great blue folio sheets, describing their lives in detail, I still lament my inability to find the love letters of another Lunar man, the eccentric Thomas Day. The radical, Rousscau-obsessed Day was famous – or notorious – for (thankfully doomed) attempts to shape two foundling girls into the perfect wife. In the end, his friends did find him a perfect wife, the heroic Esther Milnes from Wakefield, but their courtship remains a mystery. I would like more than anything to know how Day wooed her and, even more, what Esther thought.

This is one of those doors that biographers have to leave ajar if they are ever to finish. Others may unravel the true story. Letters may still turn up under the floorboards. A descendant may open the chest in the attic. And sometimes answers to baffling questions *do* turn up, in hidden corners of the very archives that we think we know well, often in a casual PS at the end of a letter. In one huge archive, that of the Darwin Project in Cambridge, I was checking the letters of 'Susannah Darwin', meaning Sukey, Josiah Wedgwood's daughter, the wife of Erasmus Darwin's son Robert and mother of Charles. Through some error, one of Sukey's letters had been filed among papers relating to a different

Susannah Darwin, Erasmus's sister, who looked after his household and sons after his first wife died. But it was the other letters in the file, which I would not otherwise have asked for, that really intrigued me – an emotional correspondence between Darwin's sons from his first marriage. They were concerned about the meanness of their late aunt's memorial, implying some neglect on the part of Darwin and his glamorous second wife, Elizabeth Pole. As I saw how important Susannah had been in their lives, I saw too that I had unthinkingly followed Darwin in ignoring her and taking her for granted.

Sometimes it almost feels as if my subject or one of their relations is raising a sardonic eyebrow at my presumption. Just when I think I have the book organized and am being coolly 'objective', a manuscript nudges my elbow, and I find I know nothing at all. The sharpest of these moments concerned Elizabeth Gaskell and a Wedgwood of a later generation, the lively, sociable Fanny, wife of Hensleigh Wedgwood. I knew that she and Elizabeth shared confidences and gossip and were, as far as I could see, the closest of friends. In the Wedgwood archives at Keele, I was happily going through the letters of the women of the family, which were then simply stored in boxes, folded in three in the old style, with the address on one side. Suddenly I was faced with the dark, spiky writing of Fanny's daughter Snow – and as I smoothed out the letter I felt myself grow hot, as if I were not doing calm historical research but overhearing something about myself that I would definitely rather not know. Fanny was in a bad mood, Snow wrote, because Mrs G. was coming to stay 'and you know she can't stand her'.

My skin prickled at this betrayal. But could it be true? As I read more of Snow's letters, almost dreading unfolding them, I found that angry sneering was a favourite tone. But the moment was salutary, because it undercut all my pretence at objectivity, and showed how dangerously close I was to identifying with my subject. So now, every time I begin to congratulate myself on getting things in order, I remember Snow's letter and am grateful.

Jane Ridley

Tarts

I knew that I wanted to write, but didn't know how to start. So I stayed on at Oxford after taking my history degree and became a graduate student at Nuffield College. This was the temple of the social sciences, dedicated to Harold Wilson's white heat of technology, and by the mid-1970s it was suffering from burnout. It was housed in a drab mock-Tudor quad on a site which had been chosen allegedly because of its closeness to Oxford station. At Nuffield, historians like me were despised as 'soft', and admitted on sufferance because we needed to be taught how to use punch cards (these were the days of card-index research), how to calculate electoral swing and party alignment or do prosopographical analysis (punch cards again). Outside the seminars where the politicians came down from London to speak off the record, the talk was mainly about job adverts in the *THES*. I sneaked off and went to live secretly in London.

My thesis was on the Tory party before 1914 – probably the most right-wing subject in British history. I'm still not sure why I chose it. My supervisor was Robert Blake, Disraeli's great biographer, who was Provost of Queen's. He had mustard suede shoes, a green tweed suit and a purplish face. He was always affable, but he seemed somehow (to use one of his favourite words) baffled. He would grumble that he couldn't read my writing, and there would be much fumbling with different pairs of spectacles. Being vain about my spidery script and rapidograph pen, I hadn't learned to type; but I began to suspect that Blake wasn't reading the stuff anyway. (A venial sin, as I know now, being a supervisor myself.) One morning I arrived at Queen's feeling dazed and shaky, having driven too fast down the A40 from London and spun my orange Mini into a scary skid of 360 degrees – only to be informed by the provost's secretary that the great man had left, having forgotten my appointment. This was probably just as well in the circumstances, but having nearly killed myself (literally) to get there, I felt somehow cheated.

The end came at a graduate history seminar in All Soul's. Blake was giving the paper – I think it was about Lord Derby. On these occasions the presenter would read a densely argued piece in a snarling monotone, dropping the voice into an ironic sneer at the end of the sentence. Blake was looking flustered and he had no typescript. In fact, he had just come down from London on the train and jotted a few notes, and the young dons tore him to pieces. That did it for me. I changed supervisors.

The trouble with Blake, I thought, was that he wasn't a 'real' historian, just a biographer. Biography seemed to me an amateur subject for non-academics who were often women of an older generation – C. V. Wedgwood, Cecil Woodham-Smith. I wanted to write revisionist articles bristling with footnotes like my historian heroes, who published in the *Historical Journal* or the *English Historical Review*.

Two decades on, I published a biography of the *Young Disraeli*. Blake gave it a generous review, which was decent of him (perhaps he never knew the reason for my defection). I can see now that Blake's *Disraeli* is still the best single life of the man – ambitious, large-minded and mildly ironic. I would class it as one of the great historical biographies of the twentieth century, along with Elizabeth Longford's *Victoria R. I.*, published two years before *Disraeli* in 1964, which still sparkles 40 years on.

My shift from would-be historian to biographer happened partly by accident. I was never much good at writing academic history. My thesis, constructed laboriously from index cards and scissors-and-paste, took 11 years to finish, and that was not from lack of trying. The only bits that flowed were the parts about people and the narrative sections. And then I discovered that no one wanted to publish that sort of thing anyway. Nudged by my agent, I moved towards biography and signed a contract for a life of Disraeli.

The Disraeli book was written in a publishing race with the prolific American biographer Stanley Weintraub. Of course, Weintraub hit the tape before me – and his was a full biography while I only did half the distance, stopping when Dizzy reached his 40s. I vowed never again to write in a race. Far more important, I discovered that biography was what I liked doing best.

I set to work to read through Dizzy's early novels. Most of these are forgotten, and rightly so, but they are a gift to his biographer. My second son was born while I worked on the book and, like a Victorian matron lying in, I took to my bed for weeks, snatching gobbets of *Alroy* or the *Young Duke* whenever the baby slept. I nearly named him Endymion after one of Disraeli's heroes – a moniker for which he probably wouldn't have thanked me. Writing about human relationships and emotions was a liberation after the years I had spent hopelessly trying to nail down elusive social trends with historical clichés. At last I had stumbled into the place where I was comfortable as a writer – the biographer's space where the public meets the private.

I was hooked. I never wanted to write another word of academic history. Every time I agreed to write a learned article or conference paper, I bitterly regretted it. Like Lord Blake, I find myself ad-libbing at seminars or conferences where formal papers are expected. I'm fortunate to teach at Buckingham, the only university in Britain which is outside the research assessment exercise. I'm under no pressure to churn out the learned articles that other historians need to produce, and I've given up all ambition of getting another job, let alone being head-hunted. My CV languishes, but I'm allowed to engage in such unprofessional conduct as spending seven years on the life of Lutyens – who, as an architect, is strictly outside my field.

I suspect that some 'real' historians still see biographers as the tarts of the profession, obsessed by sex and almost as despicable as the much-reviled (and envied) telly historians. Occasionally academic historians publish bad-tempered pieces about the uselessness of political biography, griping about the huge publisher's advances biographers receive. If only they knew. But academic attitudes are softening. The astonishing success of the *Oxford DNB* project in mobilizing academic talent and goodwill is symptomatic of a willingness to engage with individual lives that would have been unthinkable in the bad old days of Marxism.

Being a biographer does you no favours in the academic job market, but it doesn't make you a pariah among historians. When I set up an MA programme in Biography, I found that the historians whom I asked to act as examiners were always positive and supportive.

I enjoy teaching biography. It works as an MA subject because it embraces an eclectic range of subjects and the students are engaged and committed – the most exciting discussions I've had as a teacher have been with groups of biographers. But I'm ambivalent about biography becoming part of the academic mainstream. One of the chores that academics have to perform is to submit to the grilling of the Quality Assessment Audit. This involves completing countless forms specifying such things as learning and teaching outcomes and transferable skills. Filling in the boxes for the Biography MA made me realize just how different biography is from the routine history courses I teach. Of course there are skills and techniques and a literature that can be taught. But the notion of an academic template for biography worries me. Biography is a fluid, hybrid form, part art, part graft; it thrives on gossip and irony, and its vitality depends upon its freedom. I rather hope that biography will continue to float free, on the edge, between the sheets, in secret places – and that academia will never make an honest woman of biography.

Miranda Seymour

The Hand from the Grave

It doesn't surprise me that a fierce storm has exploded tonight, as
I sit down to write about the most unnerving of my experiences
as a biographer. Nothing, where Laura Riding is concerned,
seems to happen without drama.

I knew nothing about Riding when I undertook to write the
biography of Robert Graves, other than that she was an American
poet with whom he lived and who had famously leapt from a
high window in Hammersmith in 1929, seemingly under the
impression that she could fly. She survived, and they left for a
new life in Mallorca at the end of that summer.

Riding was dead when I began my researches; her literary
executors had imposed an embargo on her papers which made
research unusually difficult. It was lucky for me that her own first
biographer had taken copious notes before Riding, enraged by an
imprudent inquiry about her occult powers, decided to sever
contact. Deborah Baker was generously prepared to share her
discoveries; sympathetic archivists, while unable to show me the
original documents, let me rifle through their detailed record
cards and draw information from them.

Interviews with people who had known Riding were not
reassuring. One old lady told me that Miss Riding had taken the
place of Christ in her mind; another, whose husband had briefly
fallen under the spell of Riding's charismatic personality, was
convinced that she had links with the devil. Graves's private
secretary agreed to embark on a correspondence with me only on
condition that Laura Riding's name was never to be mentioned.
Riding was, in fact, the principal subject of his voluminous and

revealing letters. His comments, while loyal, did nothing to dispel my sense that Graves's companion had been a demanding and unpredictable woman.

The most disturbing account of her behaviour came from one of Graves's younger children. Catherine Graves was a child of 7, living on a barge at Hammersmith with her mother, while Graves and Riding lived in a nearby maisonette at St Peter's Square, when she decided to pay her father an afternoon visit. Riding answered the door and told her that Graves was busy; instead, she was invited to Riding's workroom and beckoned to sit by the open window. Outside, a spring tree rustled its leaves. Each leaf, Riding told the startled child, hid a magical sweet; if she stepped on the sill and reached out, she could take one. A magical staircase would rise to protect her from falling. All she needed to do was to believe.

Catherine Graves and I were drinking tea in the cafeteria of Barkers' department store in Kensington as she told me this extraordinary story, and how, terrified, she ran away back to the barge and never told her mother because Riding threatened her with a policeman in the sky who would come down to punish her if she ever dared to mention the magic tree. I liked Catherine, but she did not seem stable: could she have dreamed up such a bizarre event? It was impossible to know.

A visit to my home in London by Riding's new, official biographer – her book has not yet appeared – stiffened my resolve to give as honest and objective an account as I could of the woman who had exerted such a powerful influence on Graves and who had been, so her supporters said, the victim of his thieving mind when he wrote *The White Goddess*. It would, the official biographer said mildly, be wise for me to remember which of them had been the real genius. It did not seem a good moment to say that I found most of Riding's work impenetrably obscure, while Graves was one of the most lucid writers of prose of the twentieth century.

After writing the biography, I wrote a novel based on the events which took place in the summer of 1939 when Graves and Riding visited the home of an American couple and stayed in a house on their Pennsylvania farm. By the end of the summer, the wife had been imprisoned in an asylum, Graves had suffered a nervous breakdown and Riding had departed with the husband. Encountering the couple's daughter after I had published the book, I learned that my only failing had been to underestimate the malevolent power which Riding had exerted on an increasingly bewildered and disoriented household. 'You did not', she said, 'begin to understand the terror that we felt.' And she spoke of cowering behind a bedroom door, praying for protection as she listened to Riding's footsteps on the staircase and heard her name being called. I asked what it was that had been so frightening about a small, neatly-dressed woman who liked make-up but kept her brown hair tidy with a schoolgirl's hairband, fastened with a bow. What, I asked Griselda Ohanessian, had she imagined was going to happen when Riding found her? I would have to read her own account, she told me. I did and am still at a loss. I understand only that Riding was capable of making people behave as if they were under a spell.

My novel was published and I half expected that some awful misfortune would overtake me for having written about Riding as if she was possessed of occult powers. Nothing happened. I went on to write another book. I put the disturbing Laura Riding out of my thoughts, as part of the past to which I had no wish to return.

Five years later, I was given a present, an Egyptian scarab ring. The fact that it had belonged to Riding intrigued me; rashly, I decided to wear it. Five months later, I rang up the ring's donor and asked her advice. My adored husband had suddenly left me; I had been subjected to a massive tax investigation; my car had been stolen; my mother had been told she had cancer; my dog had died of a heart attack; the list of my misfortunes seemed unending. Could it, I asked, have anything to do with the ring? And if so, could I please give it back?

The kindly old lady who had given me this strange present was horrified. Surely, she said, I had not been wearing it? She herself had hung it on a twig in her garden; she would never have dreamed of keeping it in the house. I asked, as politely as I could, why she had chosen to give me such a dangerous present without adding this warning. She was convinced that she had; I was equally sure that she had not. But now, since she herself had always claimed to have occult powers – of a friendly kind – I thought it fair to ask that they should be invoked to undo some of the damage. She promised to do her best.

The ring was, at her suggestion, despatched to join a collection of gravesiana at St John's College, Oxford, where I hope it will cause no further harm. As for me, my good fortune returned as soon as it was out of my hands. As far as my writing career goes, I have taken one irrevocable decision. I will never again, so long as I live, undertake to write about Laura Riding or to accept mysterious gifts without knowing their history.

Postscript

In 1926, Robert Graves and his wife Nancy Nicholson travelled to Egypt with four children, a young nanny – and Laura Riding. The plan was for Graves and Riding to work together on a study of modernist poetry while he taught English at the University of Cairo. They intended to spend three years in Egypt; they returned to England after just four months. It was during this period that Graves gave Laura a present of a scarab ring. He also wrote a curious story, 'The Shout', in which a married couple are threatened by a character possessed of supernatural powers. The triangle of their relationship appears to echo the 'Trinity' which was established in Cairo and which ended, back in England, in a broken marriage. Writing an epilogue to *Goodbye To All That* in 1929, Graves described the formation of the Trinity as

> a unity to which you [Riding] and I pledged our faith and she [Nicholson] her pleasure. How we went together to the land where the dead parade the streets and there met with demons and returned with the demons still treading behind.

Revising the book in 1957, Graves deleted this passage. Nobody has ever been clear about its meaning. Demons can usually be dismissed with a smile. In this case, I'm willing to believe that something terrible did take place in Egypt – and that the scarab ring, if rings could speak, would tell us what it was.

Claire Harman

Who Is Sylvia?

There is a strong sense of trangression, in all its meanings, in the process of researching the life of another person. The kind of attention and effort one devotes to it, the obsessive pursuit of data and peripheral information is greater than anyone (apart from an aristocrat, perhaps) would ever devote to their own history. As a consequence, you get to know your subject's life in a way they never did. You know their great-grandparents' birth dates, the middle names of their schoolmasters, the date at which their final illness commenced. And as the picture builds up, so the biographer feels more and more omniscient: having read not only the subject's diaries and love letters, wills and shopping lists, but everyone else's connected with the story too, he feels in a unique position to judge the facts of the case, knowing so much about it.

This sense of having special knowledge often promotes fanciful identifications between the biographer and his or her subject. It is a dominant theme in fictions about biography, which usually show a researcher falling under a sort of spell, having his or her personality taken over by that of the subject. A. S. Byatt's *Possession* is a sentimental example, where one of the characters, having been drawn to study the work of an obscure nineteenth-century woman poet, discovers an actual blood connection between herself and the subject, surely the ultimate biographer's fantasy. Henry James's short story of 1899, 'The Real Right Thing', takes a more critical approach: in it, the young biographer character, George Withermore, is preparing to write the life of a recently dead author whose work he has idolized. He is overcome by the thrill and honour of being left alone with the dead man's papers, but the more the biographer goes into the archive, the greater is his sense of wrong-doing: he feels the writer's ghost straining forward and 'making dim signs out of his horror', and – not surprisingly – takes this as a sign that he should give up the project.

James's own anxieties about becoming the subject of a biography are fully evident in that story, as in others, such as *The Aspern Papers*, which ends with the destruction of Jeffrey Aspern's love letters by Miss Tina, who blithely says to the stricken scholar, 'What was I to keep them for?' The Miss Tina standpoint is not necessarily a philistine one – the narrator of the story notes (just before he hears the news about the papers) that she has somehow acquired 'the force of soul' and Miss Tina herself refers to the burning as having done 'the great thing'. Other Miss Tinas in literature are often depicted directly or indirectly preserving the integrity of the past, such as the great man's lover in Auden's poem 'Who's Who' who astonishes critics by keeping none of the subject's 'long marvellous letters'.

I'm glad now that I didn't meet the subject of my first book, Sylvia Townsend Warner, who died four years before I was asked to write her biography. It meant she never got the chance to dislike me or disapprove of my appointment, whereas I was rewarded by what Withermore in 'The Real Right Thing' describes as 'the possibility of an intercourse closer than that of life'. Warner displayed admirable fatalism about her posterity, destroying a few papers, leaving in order the love letters she wanted published, pretty much neglecting everything else. She left no instructions about her diaries but must have guessed that someone would think them publishable one day; all the same, I felt extremely intrusive when I began to read them. Sylvia was one of what Michael Holroyd calls 'the warm dead'; I was the first person to go through her papers, which had been removed by the trustees from her house (still occupied by a friend of the deceased) and stored in an attic at the Dorset County Museum. The museum had a bit of a problem, it seemed, with bequests. The works of Elizabeth Muntz, sculptress, had also been left them at approximately the same time and whenever I tried to get up the back stairs to the garret where the Warner archive was housed, more and more Muntz seemed to have strayed onto the landings.

I had come across Warner's work originally in a way that emphasized this aura of neglect, finding a package of her poems under a desk in the publisher's office where I worked in 1979. They had been left to the publisher by the author, but 18 months after Warner's death, no one had yet done anything about them. The only thing that had sent me under the desk in the first place was one of those odd hormonal rushes of late pregnancy that impel women to meet severe cleaning challenges, but when I took the poems home (I had never heard of Warner), I found the material so unusual and puzzling that by the time I went into labour a few weeks later, the book I took with me was *Lolly Willowes*, one of only three Warner novels then in print. By the middle of the next year, I was totally engrossed with the subject, had bought as many first editions as possible, had contacted the estate, the friends, put together a celebration of her work, edited the poems, changed the subject of my PhD. I was delighted when Warner's executors asked me to write the biography, of course, but also rather intimidated. Up to this point I had been studying Warner (a writer who had entirely evaded the canon); researching her life and making judgements about her personality would be an entirely different matter.

It was at this point that I began to have access to the things in the garret, the photos and love tokens, diaries and letters, books and dolls, old gardening shoes, the death mask (creepily waiting to peek-a-boo from a shoe box). No one else was the least bit interested in them at that date, and of course after a while, I felt that they were somehow meant for me, that I was a sort of self-appointed granddaughter to this childless woman, the keeper of the flame. Within a short time I could recognize, from references in the diaries, the significance and provenance of many of the objects in the collection, and turning to the job-lot of supposedly worthless books from the Frome Vauchurch library (acquired for me by a watchful dealer) found that the Prayer Book I had bought was the very one, embossed on the spine with the name 'Mrs Johnson', that Sylvia and her beloved Valentine used to do *sortes Virgilianae* in when they were first in love. Inside the book was a tear-off calendar slip used as a bookmark: 12 January 1932. I knew what this date commemorated, and that no other living person would know it. Such things certainly encourage the *Possession* factor. No 'ghosts making dim signs out of their horror' for me: if anything, I felt led on and encouraged. Even the death mask seemed to be smiling.

I was aware at the same time of a profound impertinence, especially in my necessary approaches to the many friends who had survived Sylvia. For a start, I looked wrong – or unlikely. I was only 24; married, a mother once over, pregnant with my second child. As I waddled up the drive of Sylvia's house at Frome Vauchurch in a rose-patterned maternity dress with puff sleeves, carrying the two milk bottles I had found by the gate, I was conscious of presenting a mildly ludicrous picture to the woman inside the house, looking out from behind the curtains as she always did. When I say 'I must have' I really mean I know I did, as the curtain-twitcher later told the woman who was to be her last lover that the position in which I was carrying the milk bottles, one under each pregnant breast, she found inexpressibly comical.

The lady in the house had a mischievous disposition, and

enjoyed making me uncomfortable, serving me an aspic for tea that contained mostly cat hair (the aspic itself I now suspect was a joke reference to the processes of biography), answering questions with a prolonged, silent stare. Her mild aggressiveness was understandable enough. Natasha Spender, widow of the poet, has written from bitter experience of the position in which friends and family of biographical subjects, faced with a letter from an unknown researcher, find themselves: 'It is better to grant an interview to this stranger, about whose motives, intelligence and goodwill they can as yet know nothing, and whose probity they must take on trust, because their own knowledge can contribute to the truth of the book, and truth is preferable.' The things that Sylvia's friends told me rarely, if ever, had much value for my research (unless they kept to data, which none did); the function of my visits to them was social rather than biographical, and the unspoken subject not Sylvia's secrets but whether or not I was a suitable custodian of them. Since that choice had already been made by the estate, both the friends and I had to live with it, and while most of them were more than gracious about the situation, generous with their friendship, trust and memories, others gave off signals of suspicion and suffrance that you could have cut with a cake-fork.

I stayed in the deathbed, I acquired some books, some furniture, many kind friends, but I always knew the special relationship with Sylvia Townsend Warner would date and fade. Back at Frome Vauchurch a real-life Miss Tina moved in who also felt destined to be a keeper of the flame – the bonfire flame – and who despatched wholesale whatever she could find in Sylvia's handwriting, believing Warner to have been a witch. Things were in flux: the Warner archive began to be catalogued; the diaries that I had felt it was a transgression, an impertinence, to open a few years before, became available in print. A literary society was formed; it performs ceremonies around the grave on the anniversary of Warner's death.

The first biographer of a subject forms the story, establishes the shape of the life. With a subject who is recently dead, you also generate material through the soliciting of reminiscences and opinions and begin, almost inevitably, to interact with the story yourself. Even before my book was finished, I noticed my own handwriting in the Chatto & Windus archive at Reading University – letters I had written to Norah Smallwood, Sylvia's publisher, that had already become a part of the story I was trying to uncover. I was suddenly aware of the barrier between life and life writing, but which side was I on?

The most affecting of the photographs I brought back from Samoa when researching my most recent book on Robert Louis Stevenson, was the one showing the verandah on which he died, with my own sandals in the foreground, obediently removed on the instructions of the museum's staff. There is something innocent and untainted about their presence. Unlike the biographer, they weren't trying to insert themselves in the picture. They got onto that verandah meaninglessly, like things in Stevenson's past, and I look at those sandals now with a sort of jealousy.

T. J. Binyon

Feeling Byronic

The genesis of my biography of Pushkin can be traced back to the afternoon of a hot summer's day some 50 years ago. I was then an 18-year-old National Serviceman, a radar operator in a heavy anti-aircraft battery stationed near Knutsford, in Cheshire. Whereas in training camp the loudspeakers in the barracks had issued only barked commands, here they played nothing but Radio Luxembourg, and all through the summer months Doris Day had been yearning for the Black Hills of Dakota. That afternoon began like any other: I'd started up the radar set's generator, and was sitting in my little green caravan, twiddling the saucer-shaped aerial on its roof and scanning the screen for any high-flying raiders that might be winging their way across the Irish Sea to rain high explosives on the leafy lanes of Cheshire. In a little while I'd turn on the interior light and start reading a magazine. Suddenly there was a bang on the metal door, and a disembodied voice yelled that I was wanted in the battery office. A few minutes later the sergeant-major was telling me that I had been posted to the Joint Services School of Linguists in Bodmin to learn Russian. The tone of his voice, as he announced this astonishing news, nicely expressed the view, first, that he didn't believe the unit existed, and second, that if it did, it was not part of the proper army, not the kind of place where one blancoed one's kit every day, stiffened one's folded blankets with pieces of cardboard, ironed box pleats into one's battledress, and bulled one's boots to unbelievable shininess with a heated teaspoon and the handle of one's toothbrush.

He was wrong on the first count, right on the second: normal army life was hardly possible in a camp where Russian émigrés strolled languidly into the classrooms, their overcoats slung elegantly over their shoulders, smoking cigarettes cut in half – in imitation of a Russian *papirosa* – in long amber holders, or combed their luxuriant, cavalry officer's moustaches while initiating us into the mysteries of the Russian verbal system, or, in a moment of nostalgia, confided to us that they had been so much in love in October 1917 that they hadn't noticed the revolution. But, for the next 18 months, first in Bodmin, then in London, and finally in Crail, in Fife, they force-fed us Russian with amazing success. Though, given that we were being trained as translators and interpreters for the services, there was a pettifogging insistence on acquiring a recondite military vocabulary and a detailed knowledge of the Soviet armed forces, the instructors were at the same time only too eager to introduce us to Russian literature, to Russian culture, to initiate us into that world where 'the Russian spirit is . . . there it smells of Russia', as Pushkin puts it in the prologue to his early narrative poem *Ruslan and Lyudmila*.

All this was a revelation to me, and I found it extraordinarily fascinating. To begin with, there was something satisfying about the way the parts of the Russian language fitted together, while even the most ordinary of words sounded so mysteriously attractive. And the literature was amazingly rich. Like other adolescents, I found the febrile, psychologically intense world of Dostoevsky hypnotically irresistible, and after a few chapters of *Crime and Punishment* or *The Devils* would wander around in a kind of dazed, Dostoevskian dream. Tolstoy's all-embracing universe, Turgenev's quiet pessimism and the manifold variety of Pushkin's genius were only fully appreciated later.

Earlier I had not given much thought to my future life, other than vaguely considering, without any real conviction, various professions such as law, diplomacy, business. But at this point my path suddenly became clear to me. It would have to run through literature, and specifically Russian literature. When, a year later, I left the army and went to university it was to study not my original choice, history, but Russian; at the end of the course I spent a year at Moscow University; and, a little later, began teaching Russian literature, first at the University of Leeds, and then at Oxford.

Gradually, however, towards the end of the 1980s a measure of disillusionment set in. This was partly due to external circumstances: the short-sighted niggardliness with which successive governments treated the universities induced a kind of despairing cynicism, as I found that, instead of encouraging my brightest pupils to embark on research and enter the profession, I was constrained, in all honesty, to warn them against it. And, on a personal level, I had become dissatisfied with that branch of Russian literature on which I had specialized: the Symbolist poets of the late nineteenth and early twentieth centuries. I was tired of their endless childish quarrels, their showy decadent posturing, and, worst of all, I had come to suspect – difficult though it is to evaluate the quality of verse written in a foreign language – that their work was, at the best, no more than second-rate. Under these circumstances, an interest in crime fiction, which had begun as a hobby, slowly began to occupy a larger place in my life. I had written two novels – not detective stories or thrillers, but of the kind which John Buchan, referring to *The Thirty-Nine Steps* and *Greenmantle*, termed 'shockers' – a short history of the fictional detective, and had been asked to write the official biography of the crime novelist Ngaio Marsh. I turned this down, somewhat snobbishly telling my agent, who had suggested the idea, that if I were going to write a literary biography I'd rather have a writer I admired as its subject – 'such as Pushkin', I added jokingly. A few weeks later he produced a contract for a biography of the poet.

Progress at first was slow: this was my first essay at biography, and I had no idea how to go about it, other than the vague feeling that it would be sensible to begin at the beginning and go on to the end. The first drafts of the early chapters were encumbered with unnecessary material, moved at a snail's pace and, worst of all, gave no feeling of Pushkin's self. But then, when the young Pushkin, exiled to the south of Russia, was sulkily going to parties wearing transparent muslin trousers without underwear, and clambering about the Caucasus feeling Byronic, the perspective suddenly changed. The narrative gained rhythm and an ever-increasing forward momentum. And Pushkin came sharply into focus as a fascinating yet infuriating character. A sublime poet, a writer of genius, a brilliant literary critic, he was a loyal friend, an adoring father and a loving husband. At the same time he was excessively touchy, quarrelsome, belligerent, lecherous, dissipated, feckless and improvident, not overly scrupulous in money matters, hopelessly addicted to gambling, incapable of managing his finances, and a social snob. Constantly falling in love, he had an extremely low opinion of women, and, acclaimed as an apostle of social justice, was an imperialist and Great Russian chauvinist. To chronicle the final months of his life, an inexorable and tragic progression towards the fatal duel, was both hypnotically compelling and at the same time almost unbearable.

For me there was an additional bonus. Translating Pushkin, trying to do justice to the subtle nuances of his verse and the superabundant liveliness and earthiness of his letters, reanimated that passion for Russian language and literature the germ of which had been sown on that sunny afternoon in Knutsford a long time ago.

Beryl Bainbridge

Waiting for the Biographer

Nearing 70, Beryl Bainbridge is one of our most distinguished novelists. She has written 17 novels, and is currently trying to jumpstart her 18th – and her fictional voice has always combined a distinctive blend of the menacing and the ordinary. She lives in a house near Camden Town, surrounded by memorabilia from her past, and has recently been approached by a biographer, wanting to write her life. She says that 'apart from the fact that if one's dead, one won't know anything about it', she doesn't care whether a biography of her is written or not, though she would prefer that it wasn't published while she's alive. 'God, that kind of book's worthless.'

Somebody did ask fairly recently if they could write my biography, and I was pretty astounded, and wondered why anyone should want to do it, and what the point of it would be. My reaction is, 'I'm the only person who knows what it was like, so how can anyone else write it?'

So I said no. My excuse was that I have a secretary, Brendan King, and as far as the writing life goes, he knows me better than anybody, because he's been coming here for the last 15 or 16 years. I'm not sure that he's keen on the idea, but if Brendan wanted to do it, I'd have difficulty saying no.

There's a mass of material here. I've got a whole trunkful of stuff upstairs which I've tried to sell. Two girls from the British Library came round, and were very interested, they said, and were going to send someone round to assess it. But that was a year and a half ago, and I've heard nothing more. It's all up there. Letters, two huge filing cabinets full – I can't tell you the documents I've got, hidden around. My father used to write me stories called 'Professor Pig' (that was my Uncle Len), and I've hung on to those. The earliest thing I ever did, at about the age of 11, was the 'Song of the Soldier', which I wrote and illustrated, about German prisoners of war – it's a sort of poem, which I still have. Then I wrote a novel – all upstairs.

And then there are the drafts of novels. I used to type them out on a portable typewriter: lots of badly typed script and notebooks. And there's research material as well. When I did a book about a 1870s murderer called Watson [*Watson's Apology*, 1984], I got hold of the letters he'd written from prison, from the Home Office. And I did have various copies of birth certificates of the Hitler family for my novel *Young Adolf*.

I don't mind my archive going to a public institution. I've always told my children everything that's happened to me. At least I think I have. I haven't kept anything secret. I find it very odd that some people I'm quite close to think that you should keep things secret. I don't understand that. A. N. Wilson, for instance, disagrees. He says there are things you don't tell your children. I find that odd. Though I can't say that my children are very interested. I don't know whether any of them will end up writing about me. Rudi [her younger daughter] may.

You've never been tempted to write an autobiography?
No, because in most of my early books that's all I was ever attempting – trying to understand myself. I'm really not very good at fiction. It's always me and the experiences I've had. When I was younger I wanted to write about what had happened to me as a child. You contain it in a plot, but then track back to the way your life was, with the details of your parents and aunts and uncles and, in my case, my brother. Trying to understand why it had been the way it was. Dickens fascinates me in the impact his

childhood had on his writing life. He was a very clever boy, but taken out of school and put into the blacking factory. I went to look at it the other day. It's still there in Chandos Place. There's a plaque up to him. Now he started to write because he couldn't understand why they had done that to him.

I don't think, being female, that if I'd had a so-called bland kind of childhood, I'd have ever got started. I'd have just got married and had children. But because it wasn't like that, that's *the only reason I wrote*. I would have been completely eaten up with bitterness if I hadn't started writing. I first tried to write it down when I was 11, but I was so scared that my parents would see what I'd written. I kept it in diary form and then I burnt it, in the bins at the back door. It was a beautiful book of the Travels of Livingstone, decorated with gold leaf, and I stuck a blank page in with flour and water and wrote: 'They were shouting again last night.'

It's not that I had a very peculiar upbringing, but my childhood was governed by the fact that I spent it with two people who'd been disappointed. They'd married the wrong person, failed in business, or been manipulated by others. It was set in motion before I was born. In 1929 when my brother arrived, there was the slump. Before that, my family had been quite well off. Then they lost everything. My father had been what you call a whizzkid, and my mother had married him on the rebound. After he lost his money she became very bitter, and we ended up in a house in Formby, outside Liverpool, paid for by my mother's father, Mr Baines. Whether it was my father's influence or my mother's, I don't know, but one of them was very keen on the education of their children, despite the fact that ostensibly there was no money to pay for it (my father was a bankrupt, though this was kept hidden from us). My brother had Latin tutors and piano teachers. I went to tap-dancing and elocution lessons. Where all the money came from I just don't know.

I adored my mother, but then she seemed to turn on me because I was an adolescent. She seemed to me to be selfish – but that's her generation, that's how she was brought up. My mother was fantastic to me before I went through puberty. You can't blame her for that. She was a product of her time.

How easy is it going to be for your biographer to identify the real people in your books?
[*Laughs*] I shouldn't think it's going to be easy at all. All the women are a mixture of me: the nicer ones to whom bad things happen are me; the not so nice are my mother. Ossie, my ex-husband, only comes into one book – *Another Part of the Forest*. My solicitor, who worked for Duckworth, Clive, he's in *Injury Time* and *Winter Garden*. *Watson's Apology* contains bits of my father. My brother is very much in *A Quiet Life*. I could write a list. My auntie Margot – she's in *The Dressmaker* – with my auntie Nellie. I think I swapped them round as to who is the Dressmaker. *A Weekend with Claud* was about a man who owned an antique shop in Tring, who I met in Hampstead when I first came to London. Even *Young Adolf* is set in Liverpool, with all the streets I remembered, and the people I knew.

Harriet Said, the first novel I wrote, but the third one that was published [in 1972], was originally described by one publisher as repulsive beyond belief. It was based on a friend of mine who lived down the road, and a man I met who I went to Paris with when I was 16 – and funnily enough in the new novel, which I've stopped, I'm about to go to Paris with a man. We had to forge a passport so I could go. He was a business friend of my father's and lived near us. He seemed to me to be about 60, but I suppose he was 40. It sounds a bit daft, but I can't remember whether we had an affair. On the aeroplane to France we sat next to some government minister and his and my seatbelt got mixed up, and the minister turned and said to this man, 'Don't worry about your daughter.' When we got to Paris we didn't have to go in through customs, and just got into this minister's car. At the hotel, I do remember the woman at the desk saying, 'Courage, Mademoiselle', as we were going upstairs. That's the first novel.

You grow old – and you write and you write and you write – and you don't live any more. And that's why in my later novels I had to turn to historical events and real-life subjects.

I think if anyone writes my biography, the greatest problem he or she will face lies in understanding the vastly different social background that existed during the earlier part of my life. It was a different world. There was a class system. People like me, who came from Liverpool, had to make a leap out of that class structure in a way that just doesn't happen any more. For me to have left school at 14, and then find myself, when I was working at Duckworth, mixing with people like Freddie Ayer, was extraordinary. Of course, I didn't understand half of what he was saying.

But you're not worried about any revelations that may emerge when someone publishes a biography of you?
No, why should I? I'll be dead. If there is anything I'm ashamed of, it's very early on, when I didn't know enough and was too young to cope. For instance, I think I was too young to understand my son. I think I was a bad mother to my son, but I've made amends since. But I was left very young with children. But generally, no I don't think I've treated people badly. In fact just the reverse. I think in many ways I've been a masochist and enjoyed it. I quite liked people treating *me* badly – or I used to when I was young. I always remember as a child in class at school, when somebody was asked to own up, I would be first on my feet. And yet I knew nothing about it. But I loved owning up. I quite liked that.

Oh, but there is something else I feel awful about, and that's the way I treated my cats. Gerald Duckworth and Pudding both lived to about the age of 21 and for the last six years I used to keep them outside. They'd sit on the windowsill, look in, and I used to throw food at them. Now I feel bad about that.

Biographies

Beryl Bainbridge is the author of 17 novels, two travel books, and five plays for stage and television. Her novel *Every Man for Himself* (1996) was awarded the Whitbread Novel of the Year Award and was shortlisted for the Booker Prize. She won the *Guardian* Fiction Prize with *The Dressmaker* (1973), and the Whitbread Prize with *Injury Time* (1977). Her latest novel is *According to Queeney* (2002).

T. J. Binyon is the author of *Pushkin: A Biography* (2002), winner of the Samuel Johnson Prize for Non-Fiction, and shortlisted for the *Los Angeles Times* 2004 Book Prize for Biography. He taught Russian Literature at Oxford, where he was a university lecturer and a Senior Research Fellow at Wadham College.

Mark Bostridge won the Gladstone Memorial Prize at Oxford University. His books include *Vera Brittain: A Life* (1995), which was shortlisted for the Whitbread Biography Award, the NCR Prize for Non-Fiction and the Fawcett Prize, and *Letters from a Lost Generation* (1998). He is writing a biography of Florence Nightingale.

Margaret Forster is a prolific novelist. She is also the author of *The Rash Adventurer: the Rise and Fall of Charles Edward Stuart* (1973), *William Makepeace Thackeray: Memoirs of a Victorian Gentleman* (1978), *Elizabeth Barrett Browning: A Biography* (1988), winner of the Royal Society of Literature Award, and *Daphne du Maurier* (1993).

Antonia Fraser's most recent biography is the internationally bestselling *Marie Antoinette: The Journey* (2001) which followed *The Gunpowder Plot: Terror and Faith in 1605* (1996, winner of the CWA Non-Fiction Gold Dagger). She has also written *Mary Queen of Scots* (1969), *Cromwell, Our Chief of Men* (1973) and *Charles II* (1980), as well as a short study, *King James VI and I* (1974), in the Weidenfeld and Nicolson Kings and Queens of England series, which she edits. She has written three studies of women in history, *The Weaker Vessel* (1984), *The Warrior Queens* (1989) and *The Six Wives of Henry VIII* (1993). Among other awards, she has received the James Tait Black Memorial Prize for Biography (1969), the Wolfson Award for History (1984), the Norton Medlicott Medal (2000) of the Historical Association and the Franco-British Literary Prize (2002).

Lyndall Gordon received her doctorate from Columbia University. Before becoming a full-time writer she taught at St Hilda's College, Oxford. Her books include a two-volume biography of *T. S. Eliot* (1998), winner of the Rose Mary Crawshay Prize and the Southern Arts Prize, *Virginia Woolf: A Writer's Life* (1984), winner of the James Tait Black Memorial Prize for Biography, *Shared Lives* (1992), *Charlotte Bronte: A Passionate Life* (1994), winner of the Cheltenham Prize, and *A Private Life of Henry James: Two Women and His Art* (1998). Her two-generation biography of Mary Wollstonecraft and her heirs is published in 2005.

Claire Harman worked for the literary periodical *PN Review* in the 1980s and has brought up three children. She wrote a biography of *Sylvia Townsend Warner* (1989) which won the John Llewellyn Rhys Prize, and edited Warner's poems and diaries. Her life of *Fanny Burney* (2000) was shortlisted for the Whitbread Biography Award, and she has a biography of Robert Louis

Stevenson forthcoming in 2005. She teaches a course in biography at Columbia University in New York and lives the rest of the year in Oxford.

Brian Harrison was Editor of the *Oxford Dictionary of National Biography* from January 2000 to September 2004, and since 1963 has published several books and many articles on nineteenth- and twentieth-century British political and social history. He is now 'retired', but is completing the final volume in the *New Oxford History of England* on the period 1951–90.

Michael Holroyd has written biographies of *Lytton Strachey* (1967–8), *Augustus John* (1974–5) and *Bernard Shaw* (1988–91), and two volumes of family memoirs, *Basil Street Blues* (1999) and *Mosaic* (2004). He has been Chairman of the Society of Authors and is President of the Royal Society of Literature.

Kathryn Hughes's *George Eliot: The Last Victorian* (1998) won the James Tait Black Memorial Prize for Biography. She is currently working on a book about Mrs Beeton. She reviews for the *Guardian* and teaches life writing at the University of East Anglia.

Hermione Lee is the Goldsmiths' Professor of English Literature at New College Oxford. She is well known as a reviewer and broadcaster and has written books on Elizabeth Bowen, Willa Cather, Philip Roth and Virginia Woolf. Her biography of *Virginia Woolf* (1996) won the Rose Mary Crawshay Prize and has been translated into French, German, Korean and Polish. She is currently working on a biography of Edith Wharton and a collection of essays on life writing. She was awarded the CBE for services to literature in 2003.

Jeremy Lewis spent much of his working life in publishing, and was for ten years a director of Chatto & Windus. He was for some years the Deputy Editor of the *London Magazine*, and is now the Commissioning Editor of *The Oldie*. He has written two volumes of autobiography. His life of *Cyril Connolly* was published in 1997, and that of *Tobias Smollett* in 2003. He is currently writing a biography of Allen Lane, the founder of Penguin Books. He has written the entry on Barbara Skelton in the *Oxford Dictionary of National Biography*.

Fiona MacCarthy is the author of *Eric Gill* (1989), *William Morris: A Life For Our Time* (1994), winner of the Wolfson Prize for History and the Writer's Guild Non-Fiction Award, and *Byron: Life and Legend* (2002).

Diarmaid MacCulloch is Professor of the History of the Church at Oxford University, and a Fellow of the British Academy. His *Thomas Cranmer: A Life* (1996) was the winner of the Whitbread Biography Award, the James Tait Black Memorial Prize for Biography and the Duff Cooper Prize. His latest book is *Reformation: Europe's House Divided* (2003).

Lucasta Miller is the author of *The Brontë Myth* (2001). She has reviewed widely and is a former deputy literary editor of the *Independent*. She now writes for the *Guardian* and the *Daily Telegraph*, and is working on a cultural history of *Hamlet*. Her edition of Charlotte Brontë's *Shirley* is forthcoming from Penguin next year. She is a trustee of the London Library.

Andrew Motion is the author of *The Lamberts* (1986), *Philip Larkin: A Writer's Life* (1993), winner of the Whitbread Biography Award, *Keats* (1997), *Wainewright The Poisoner* (2000) and *The Secret of Dr Cake* (2003). He was appointed Poet Laureate in 1999.

Ben Pimlott was Warden of Goldsmiths College and the author of biographies of *Hugh Dalton* (1985), winner of the Whitbread Biography Award, *Harold Wilson* (1992) and *The Queen* (1996). He died in April 2004.

Jane Ridley is Reader in History at Buckingham University, and author of *The Young Disraeli* (1996) and *The Architect and His Wife: A Life of Edwin Lutyens* (2002), winner of the Duff Cooper Prize.

Graham Robb has written biographies of *Balzac* (1994), *Victor Hugo* (1997) which won the Whitbread Biography Award and the W. H. Heinemann Prize, and *Rimbaud* (2000). His latest book, *Strangers: Homosexual Love in the 19th Century*, was published in 2003. He is writing a book about the colonization of France.

Andrew Roberts's books include *The Holy Fox* (1991) and *Salisbury: Victorian Titan* (1999), winner of the Wolfson History Prize. He is currently writing *A History of the English-Speaking Peoples Since 1900*.

Miranda Seymour has written biographies of *Ottoline Morrell: Life on a Grand Scale* (1992) and *Mary Shelley* (2000). Her most recent book is *The Bugatti Queen: In Search of a Motor-Racing Legend* (2004). Her biography of *Robert Graves: Life on the Edge* was reissued in 2003; her novel about Graves and Riding, *The Telling*, was published in 1999.

Robert Skidelsky is the author of a three-volume biography of *John Maynard Keynes: Hopes Betrayed* (1983), *The Economist As Saviour* (1992), winner of the Wolfson History Prize, and *Fighting For Britain* (2000), winner of the Duff Cooper, Lionel Gelber, James Tait Black Memorial and Council on Foreign Relations

Prizes. He is Professor of Political Economy at the University of Warwick.

Frances Spalding has written lives of the artists *Roger Fry* (1980), *Vanessa Bell* (1987), *John Minton* (1991) and *Gwen Raverat* (2001), and of the poet *Stevie Smith* (1988). She is also an historian of twentieth-century art and the author of *British Art Since 1900* (1986) and a centenary history of the Tate (1998). She is currently writing a joint biography of John and Myfanwy Piper.

Hilary Spurling has written a two-volume life of Ivy Compton-Burnett, *Ivy When Young* (1974) and *Secrets of a Woman's Heart* (1984), winner of the Duff Cooper Memorial Prize and the W. H. Heinemann Award, *Paul Scott* (1990), *La Grande Therese: The Greatest Swindle of the Century* (1999) and *The Girl from the Fiction Department* (2002). The first volume of her life of Henri Matisse, *The Unknown Matisse*, was published in 1998. The second volume, *The Conquest of Colour*, is forthcoming in 2005.

John Sutherland is Lord Northcliffe Professor of Modern English Literature at University College London and a Visiting Professor of Literature at the California Institute of Technology. He is the author of many works of literary criticism and publishing history, and has written three biographies, *Mrs Humphry Ward* (1990), *Sir Walter Scott* (1995) and *Stephen Spender: The Authorized Biography* (2004). He writes a weekly column in the *Guardian*.

D. J. Taylor is the author of five novels, most recently *Trespass* (1998) and *The Comedy Man* (2001). His life of *Thackeray* was published in 1999 and his centenary study, *Orwell: The Life*, won the 2003 Whitbread Biography Award.

Ian Thomson's biography, *Primo Levi,* won the Royal Society of Literature W. H. Heinemann Award in 2003. His travel book, *Bonjour Blanc: A Journey Through Haiti,* was reissued in 2004 with a new preface by J. G. Ballard.

Claire Tomalin is the author of seven biographies: *The Life and Death of Mary Wollstonecraft* (1974), which won the Whitbread First Book Prize, *Shelley and His World* (1980), *Katherine Mansfield: A Secret Life* (1987), *The Invisible Woman: The Story of Nelly Ternan and Charles Dickens* (1990), winner of the Hawthornden Prize, the NCR Prize for Non-Fiction and the James Tait Black Memorial Prize for Biography, *Mrs Jordan's Profession* (1994), *Jane Austen: A Life* (1997) and *Samuel Pepys: The Unequalled Self* (2002), winner of the Whitbread Book of the Year Award and the inaugural Samuel Pepys Award. She has also published a collection of her literary journalism, *Several Strangers: Writings from Three Decades* (1999). She is currently working on a biography of Thomas Hardy.

Jenny Uglow is the author of critical studies of Henry Fielding and George Eliot, and the biographies *Elizabeth Gaskell: A Habit of Stories* (1993) and *Hogarth: A Life and a World* (1997), both shortlisted for the Whitbread Biography Award. Her group biography, *The Lunar Men* (2002), won the Hessell-Tiltman Prize for History and the James Tait Black Memorial Prize for Biography. Her most recent book is *A Little History of British Gardening* (2004).

Sara Wheeler's books include *Travels in a Thin Country: A Journey Through Chile* (1994), *Terra Incognita: Travels in Antarctica* (1996) and *Cherry: A Life of Apsley Cherry-Garrard* (2001). She is currently writing the life of Denys Finch Hatton, the English aristocrat and white hunter who fell in love with Karen Blixen (among others) in East Africa. She is the co-editor of *Amazonian: The Penguin Book of Women's New Travel Writing*.

Andrew Wilson is the author of *Beautiful Shadow: A Life of Patricia Highsmith* (2003), which was shortlisted for the Whitbread Biography Award, and was the winner of an Edgar Allan Poe Award. He is writing a biography of Harold Robbins.

Frances Wilson is the author of *Literary Seductions: Compulsive Writers and Diverted Readers* (1999) and *The Courtesan's Revenge: Harriette Wilson, the Woman Who Blackmailed the King* (2003). She teaches English Literature at Reading University.

Ann Wroe has a doctorate in history from Oxford University and is a senior editor on *The Economist*. Her biography of *Pontius Pilate* (1999) was shortlisted for the Samuel Johnson Prize and the W. H. Smith Award. *Perkin. A Story of Deception* was published in 2003.